DATE DUE

INNOVATIVE MINDS

DIAN FOSSEY

BEFRIENDING THE GORILLAS

Suzanne Freedman

RSVP
RAINTREE
STECK-VAUGHN
PUBLISHERS
The Steck-Vaughn Company

Austin, Texas

Acknowledgments

The publisher would like to thank H. Dieter Steklis, Ph.D., Scientific Director of the Dian Fossey Gorilla Fund, for his valuable help in reviewing this book.

Copyright © 1997 Steck-Vaughn Company

Published by Raintree Steck-Vaughn Publishers, an imprint of Steck-Vaughn Company.

Series created by Blackbirch Graphics
Series Editor: Tanya Lee Stone
Editor: Lisa Clyde Nielsen
Associate Editor: Elizabeth M. Taylor
Production/Design Editor: Calico Harington

Raintree Steck-Vaughn Publishers Staff
Editors: Shirley Shalit, Kathy DeVico
Project Manager: Lyda Guz

Library of Congress Cataloging-in-Publication Data

Freedman, Suzanne, 1932–
   Dian Fossey : befriending the gorillas / Suzanne Freedman.
     p.   cm. — (Innovative minds)
   Includes bibliographical references and index.
   Summary: Describes the life of the scientist and her accomplishments working with gorillas in Africa.
   ISBN 0-8172-4405-0
   1. Fossey, Dian—Juvenile literature. 2. Primatologists—United States—Biography—Juvenile literature. 3. Gorilla—Rwanda—Juvenile literature. [1. Fossey, Dian. 2. Zoologists. 3. Women—Biography. 4. Gorilla] I. Title. II. Series.
QL31.F65F74   1997
599.88'46'092—dc20
[B]
                                       96-18927
                                          CIP
                                          AC

Printed in the United States of America
1 2 3 4 5 6 7 8 9 0 LB 00 99 98 97 96

Table of Contents

Dian Fossey dedicated 18 years of her life to studying and protecting mountain gorillas.

A Most
Important
Meeting

In the spring of 1966, Dr. Louis Leakey, the world's most respected expert in paleoanthropology—the study of early humans—stopped in Louisville, Kentucky, on a lecture tour. At the time, he was 63 years of age, he suffered from arthritis, he limped, and he wheezed. But he once told a friend that he expected never to die because he had no time for it; he had too many irons in the fire. He had always been involved in ambitious research projects on several continents. Archaeological digs (undertaken to find evidence of early humans) had been led by Leakey in Tanzania, Kenya, Ethiopia, Israel, and the United States.

Leakey's interests extended to nonhuman animals as well. He thought that the mountain gorilla, an older species of great ape, needed to be studied. In 1959, he had recruited a field zoologist, George Schaller, to conduct a pioneering study of the mountain gorilla. But Leakey now felt that more research than Schaller's total of 466 hours would be needed. Schaller's research had focused mostly on range behavior— the animals' movement in their environment—not social behavior. Leakey knew that the gorilla population was dwindling, and he was looking for someone to conduct a more intensive field study while the animals still survived. He hoped to be able to find the same kind of person to work with gorillas as Jane Goodall, who had worked with chimpanzees in Tanzania for many years.

REUNION

Dr. Fred Coy was one of the few people with whom Dian Fossey had become close at Kosair Children's Hospital in Louisville, Kentucky, where she had worked as an occupational therapist since 1955. She would talk endlessly to him about the African safari that she had gone on in 1963 and how she had met the famous Dr. Louis Leakey at a dig at Olduvai Gorge, in Tanzania. So when Coy saw the announcement that Leakey would be speaking at the University of Louisville, he could hardly wait to tell Fossey. The public lecture was scheduled for Sunday, April 3, 1966, at 8:00 P.M.

Fossey resolved to seize the moment. She wanted to show Leakey the three articles that she had written for *The Louisville Courier Journal* about his fossil discoveries—and one article relating her experience with mountain gorillas on Zaire's Mount Mikeno, entitled "I Photographed the Mountain Gorilla."

Clutching her newspaper clippings, Dian Fossey sat in the rear of the university's Bigelow Hall Auditorium on the evening of the lecture. Her excitement was shared by a large audience who had come to hear Dr. Leakey tell the story of the earliest humans.

Dr. Leakey's lecture lasted three hours, and afterward, many people came up to talk to him. Fossey waited patiently at the end of a long line—as the last in line, she might be able to spend more time with him. And she had a lot to say.

When they finally were face to face, she was thrilled that Leakey remembered meeting her three years before. He looked at her articles, especially the one about mountain gorillas. What impressed Leakey most about Fossey's article was that she, unlike most tourists venturing to East Africa at that time, had managed on her own to get where the gorillas were. She had seen the gorillas, and she not only had managed to write about her experience, but she also had taken photographs of the animals.

Leakey explained that he had to leave early the next morning. Would Fossey have breakfast with him the following morning at his hotel?

They met for about half an hour, a meeting that left Fossey exhilarated by her prospects for the future. Leakey had told her that he was looking for someone to conduct an in-depth study of the mountain gorilla. He was looking for an untrained person, as he felt that trained scientists tended to see *too* much. Therefore, Leakey saw Fossey's lack of much scientific training as an advantage. What was more, Leakey believed that women were more patient than men, more sensitive to mother/child relationships, and not as likely to arouse aggression in male gorillas.

Fossey did not have the money to fund such work, she had no training in the "ologies"—zoology, anthropology, and so on—and she felt that at age 34, she was too old to undertake such a project. Louis Leakey, though, argued that, at her age, she had gained a maturity that would be invaluable in studying the mountain gorillas.

In 1959, Dr. Louis Leakey discovered a prehistoric skull of a species, which he claimed to be a direct ancestor of humans. Even though he was famous for his anthropological studies, Leakey encouraged scientific study of living, nonhuman animals.

Dian Fossey

Just as the interview was about to end, Leakey asked if Fossey had had her appendix out. She found this a strange question, but Leakey explained that many people working in remote regions had appendicitis attacks, could not get medical help in time, and suffered lingering deaths. Leakey's wife, Mary, and one of his assistants had both suffered appendicitis attacks in the bush and had nearly died.

Dian Fossey was so eager to be selected by Leakey that she would have done nearly anything to show her determination—but she was not exactly prepared to have a major operation. At least, not yet.

A month passed, but Fossey received no word from Dr. Leakey. She finally wrote him that she had read and practically memorized George Schaller's two books on gorillas. She said that she was learning how to speak Swahili, the major language of the regions where the gorillas lived. She had not yet quit her job, though—and she had not had her appendix removed. Two weeks later, Leakey wrote that he had nothing definite yet to offer Fossey. He made mention of an appendectomy. On June 8, Fossey wrote Leakey that she intended to have her appendix removed in three weeks unless he cabled her otherwise—collect.

Finally, a week later, Leakey came up with a plan. He would pay Fossey's expenses for a trip to Africa, the cost to employ one or more African staff, and a small salary. He had to raise the money, though—possibly from private sources, and possibly from the National Geographic Society. In exchange, Fossey would publish articles and photographs in *National Geographic* magazine, and would lecture and write books to bring in income. Fossey should send him a résumé summarizing her education and work experience, he said, and a report of her experience with the gorillas in 1963.

"The Black Man with a White Face"

At the entrance to the National Museum of Kenya in Nairobi stands a bronze statue of Dr. Louis Leakey. He is dressed in baggy coveralls. He is not wearing socks. His shoelaces are missing. The tongues of his shoes are hanging out. He is sitting on the ground, and in one hand, he is holding a rock. This may be one of the few statues of a white man on the continent of Africa.

Louis Seymour Bazett Leakey always considered himself an African. Born in Kenya in 1903, his parents were English missionaries. Louis was raised among the Kikuyu tribe. His boyhood friends were African; there were very few other children of Europeans to play with near the mission or anywhere else in Kenya. Louis Leakey spoke, thought, even dreamed in Kikuyu. When he was a teenager, he was initiated into the Kikuyu tribe. They named him Wakaruigi, "Son of the Sparrow Hawk." As an adult, he enjoyed all the privileges of a tribal elder. Kikuyu tribal chief Koinanage once said of him: "We call him the black man with a white face because he is more of an African than a European."

Leakey earned a doctorate degree in anthropology at Cambridge University and married archaeologist Mary Douglas. Together, they began an investigation of ancient ancestors of human beings. In 1959, at a dig at Olduvai Gorge in Tanzania, the Leakeys discovered the skull of a member of the species *Homo habilis,* who they claimed was the earliest toolmaker and a direct ancestor of modern man. By 1965, several other fossils had been found, including a *Homo erectus* skull about a million years old. When asked what contributed to his success as a fossil hunter, Dr. Leakey replied, "Two things. Patience...and observation...Be patient, be careful, don't hurry. Try again and again and again."

Shortly before he died, in October 1972, someone asked if he was afraid of dying. Dr. Leakey responded, "Why should I mind dying? My spirit will live on in my family...but my soul will go on forever."

The Leakey family, a celebrated dynasty of fossil hunters, is still leading the field in the search for human origins. Louis S. B. Leakey made discoveries that established East Africa as the ancestral grounds for many human forerunners. After Leakey's death, his son Richard won praise for discovering several specimens of early humans in northern Kenya. Richard's wife, Meave, is the new standard-bearer of the Leakeys. She is the head of paleontology at the National Museum of Kenya. The Leakey spirit also continues to live on in their daughter Louise, who has degrees in geology and biology and often works with her mother.

Richard and Meave Leakey examine fossils during an expedition in Kenya in 1970.

Fossey scheduled an appendectomy for June 28. If Leakey wanted her to cancel the operation, she wrote him, he should let her know at once. There was no reply. Thus, the operation was performed, which Fossey now considered a small sacrifice for a great opportunity. On the other hand, though, she could not help wondering if studying the mountain gorillas was worth such a radical action.

When Fossey returned home from the hospital, there was a letter waiting from Leakey. He wrote, "Actually, there really isn't any dire need...to have your appendix removed. That is only my way of testing applicants' determination!" But Leakey added that he was anxious to get the expedition organized, and he told her she had a job. She would hear from him again as soon as he could get the necessary funding and travel permits.

Dian Fossey was ecstatic. Now there was no question about her going to Africa. She was going to study mountain gorillas for Dr. Louis Leakey! She gave notice to the Kosair Children's Hospital with no regrets, and at the end of July, she drove to California to spend time with her parents. There, she would await further word from Leakey.

A Lonely Childhood

Dian Fossey was born in Atherton, California, on January 16, 1932. The unhappiness that seemed to trouble her much of her life began when her father and mother divorced. Dian was just three years old. Her mother, Kitty, told her that her father, George Fossey III, was dead. (After the divorce, George mysteriously disappeared.) Dian became convinced that his "death" was real.

Dian's childhood in California was a lonely and unhappy one.

Thirty years later, she discovered that he was alive and had remarried. They had an uneasy reunion. Dian had mixed feelings about her father. On the one hand, she felt that he was a misunderstood, wonderful man; on the other, she was angry that he had not treated her very well. George Fossey committed suicide in 1968. Whatever Dian's feelings were about her father's death, she chose not to share them with anyone.

Without a father, Dian looked to her mother for emotional support, but she saw little of Kitty, who worked as a fashion model for San Francisco clothing stores. One columnist for *The San Francisco Chronicle* wrote that Kitty was "the most beautiful model in the city." For the most part, Dian was left in the care of Aunt Flossie, Kitty's sister, and her uncle, Bert Chapin. Dian would remember them in later years with great affection; she would even name two gorillas after her aunt and uncle.

When Dian was five, Kitty married an ambitious businessman named Richard Price. Kitty and Richard shared a desire to be well known in the community. Tall and well dressed, Price doted on the beautiful Kitty, but he practically ignored his stepdaughter. He had strict views on raising children and did not feel that they should be included in the adult world. Dian was not allowed to join her parents at dinner until she was ten years old. Until then, she ate her meals in the kitchen with the housekeeper.

Dian, always somewhat of a loner, began to withdraw more and more into herself. She hated her stepfather and never forgave her mother for marrying him. Mother and daughter began to grow apart.

Kitty was always critical of her daughter's appearance. By the time Dian was 14, she stood 6 feet 1 inch tall, taller than

Dian's life-long love of animals would begin as an adolescent.
She particularly enjoyed spending time with horses.

everyone her own age—taller even than her parents. Dian's unusual height made Kitty uncomfortable. She always made Dian feel that she was too big, too awkward, and no great beauty.

Dian thought that she was ugly, but actually, she was quite pretty. She had thick black hair, dark eyebrows, and hazel eyes; she had small bones and delicate features that contrasted pleasantly with her height. Dian, though, wished that she looked like her petite, blond mother.

In her years at Lowell High School in Atherton, Dian spent a lot of time with horses. When she wasn't studying or in the classroom, she would spend most of her time riding. She became a member of a horseback-riding club. Dian's love of horses helped her through a difficult adolescence into young adulthood. Her ability to handle horses even got her a job one summer on a dude ranch in Montana, in 1953, the summer before her college graduation. She loved the job but had to leave when she contracted chicken pox. One of her friends there remembered Dian as being much more involved with animals than with people.

Her stepfather's business became more successful, but Dian always held a job. As a college student, she spent holidays and weekends doing clerical and laboratory work. Once she worked in a factory as a machine operator.

Dian's stepfather wanted her to seek a business career. But she had other ideas. In 1950, she enrolled at the University of California at Davis as a preveterinary medical student. She wanted to share her life with animals. During her enrollment, Dian did well in writing, art, botany, and zoology, but she could not seem to master chemistry and physics. She failed her second year in college, which forced her to abandon her first career choice.

Dian then decided that she wanted to work with handicapped children. To this end, she transferred in 1952 to San Jose State College. During her two years at San Jose, she stabled her own horse and drove her own car. But she still had a poor view of herself. Though her sorority sisters at San Jose thought she was very beautiful, Dian still did not see herself that way.

Louisville Beckons

In 1954, Dian Fossey graduated from San Jose State College with a bachelor's degree in occupational therapy. She worked for nine months at local hospitals to earn her certification (official approval) as an occupational therapist. Then she had to start looking for a job. She knew that she did not want to stay in California, but she had to find a place where she could be near animals, especially horses.

Scanning the classified advertising in the *American Journal of Occupational Therapy* one day, she found an ad for a job as an occupational therapist at the Kosair Crippled Children's Hospital in Louisville, Kentucky. This appealed to her because Kentucky was far from home and one of the major centers of the horse world. Fossey got the job, moved to Louisville in September 1955, and joined Kosair's staff of two doctors, five nurses, and ten aides. She would work at Kosair for 11 years, and it would be the only occupational therapist job she would ever have.

In the mid-1950s, Louisville was beginning to make the change from a big town to a small city. But even as it grew, it remained under the influence of old, established families and still maintained an elegant atmosphere. The Kosair

Dian posed with her mother on her graduation
day from San Jose State College in 1954.

Dian Fossey

Crippled Children's Hospital, for example, was housed in an English-type manor house, set back on a rolling green lawn surrounded by oak and flowering dogwood trees. Through the financial backing of local businesspeople, the hospital cared for the young patients without charging their parents. Many of the patients were from poor families from the mountains of eastern Kentucky. Most of the children were polio victims; the Salk vaccine was just becoming available and could not help those already struck by the disabling disease.

It took little medical training to become an occupational therapist, or OT, in the 1950s, but a qualified applicant had to have nine months of clinical training plus a college degree. OTs helped disabled patients learn to make items such as baskets and handbags. They also constructed simple braces, which allowed patients to handle a knife and fork.

Two therapists give a young polio victim a warm bath in 1952. Across the country, many children were sent to hospitals, such as Kosair, to be rehabilitated from the devastating effects of polio.

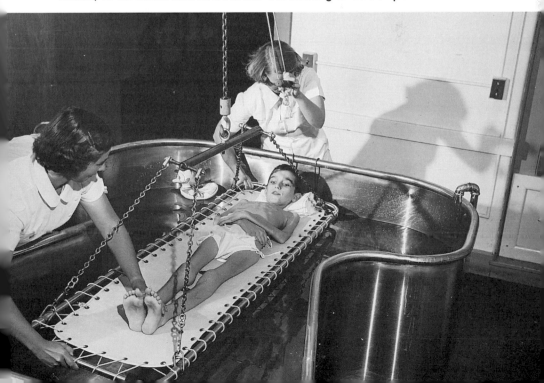

The pay was poor and the future career opportunities for occupational therapists were limited. But, fortunately for Fossey, there were more jobs for beginning OTs than there were qualified applicants in 1955.

Fossey wanted to live on her own, well away from her fellow workers at Kosair. She found a run-down cottage for rent on the Long family's century-old farm, some ten miles outside of Louisville. It had a small living room, dining alcove, bedroom, kitchen, and bath. It was called the "Washhouse" because it had been used by servants as a place to launder the clothes of attorney George Long's ancestors in the days before the Civil War. The Washhouse would be Fossey's home for the next ten years.

The Longs encouraged Fossey to help out with farm chores, and she was able to put her knowledge of veterinary medicine to good use. The Longs kept 90 or so head of Angus cattle. The farm dogs, Mitzi, Shep, and Brownie, adopted Fossey as one of their own. A big white shepherd dog would stop by for an occasional handout. At night, raccoons and opossums abounded. Dian was always on the lookout for stray animals; she fed them from food scraps that she collected at the hospital. She felt very comfortable doing these things.

Fossey had very little interest in making small talk; she kept mostly to herself. Her physical stature made it hard for her to remain unnoticed, though. One of the doctors at Kosair was heard to remark that she was somewhat unkempt. But Fossey had a natural affection for children that made it easy for her to communicate with her patients. She was compassionate when they hurt, though she was demanding of them in her role as an occupational therapist. She was tough but fair. She got results.

Fossey became especially close to Norma Kelley, a young patient at Kosair. Norma, who had been in and out of Kosair for 12 years, was 13 when they first met. The doctors had told Norma that she might never walk again. She had had four leg operations in as many years. But the fifth operation had proved successful, and she no longer had to wear braces. Norma's attachment to Kosair was so strong that she tried to get an office job there when she was 19. When a position became available in the spring of 1962, she was required to take a civil service exam in Frankfurt, some 50 miles east of Louisville. Her mother agreed to drive her there. On the way, she lost control of the car, and there was a terrible accident. Norma, seriously injured, was sent back to Kosair for surgery.

Norma recalled that every time she opened her eyes, there was Dian Fossey, standing by her bed. Norma's jaw had been broken, and Fossey fed her baby food to keep up her strength. Norma remembers Dian saying, "Why her? Why couldn't it have been me?"

THE HENRY HOTEL

Dian Fossey never went out of her way to seek friendships. She preferred to let other people decide whether or not they wanted to be her friend. Fossey had been working at Kosair for only two months when she met Mary White Henry, a secretary with whom she shared an office. Henry sensed that Fossey was just a shy person, not distant and snooty, as many of the other staff believed. Mary Henry and Dian Fossey had some things in common. They were both fond of reading. They were polite. And they were college-educated.

THE LARGEST LIVING PRIMATES

There are three subspecies of gorillas—the western lowland gorilla, the eastern lowland gorilla, and the mountain gorilla. Mountain gorillas, the largest living primates, number around 600 and are highly endangered. They cannot be found in zoos anywhere in the world. Mountain gorillas survive today in present-day Rwanda, Zaire, and Uganda. About 300 live in the Virunga Mountain region of Rwanda and Zaire. The other surviving mountain gorillas live in Bwindi National Park in Uganda. Mountain gorillas live in groups of 2 to 35 or more.

Gorillas are massive, with long, powerful arms and short, bowed legs. An adult male may weigh more than 440 pounds—about twice that of an adult female. Their faces are black, and prominent brow ridges overhang their eyes. Their bodies are well adapted to forest life. Their big toes are shaped like thumbs and are used to hang onto branches when climbing. Gorillas use their fingers and thumbs like humans do. An adult male is called a silverback, because the hair on the back of a male starts to turn silver at about age 10 to 13 years. As the center of the group, he is easy to spot. He determines travel routes, resting places, and group activities, and he protects the group from danger.

Gorillas can stand upright if they need to, though when they do, it is only for short distances. They usually walk on all fours and support their bodies on the middle knuckles of their hands. They climb into trees to get a good view, to sleep, or to look for food. Mountain gorillas eat huge amounts of vegetation, including celery, berries called gallium, roots, bark, and bamboo sprouts. These foods make up 90 percent of their diet. Silverbacks can eat as much as 75 pounds of bamboo every day. Gorillas spend about 40 percent of their day resting, 30 percent eating, and 30 percent traveling. A typical gorilla day usually begins around 8:00 A.M. when the silverback leads his group to cross-country feeding, browsing from one plant to the next, covering about 1,000 feet in two hours. The group then stops for a midday break of two to four hours, which they spend snacking, dozing, and sunbathing. Around 2:00 P.M., the group moves on again to resume feeding. They take their time and come to a stop around 5:00 P.M. Then they prepare for a night's rest by building nests in trees or on the ground. They pull tree branches together and crush them into a bed as they retire for the night.

Each female has one baby at a time. She does not have another until the first is four or five years old. Baby gorillas develop inside their mothers for eight or nine months. A baby gorilla weighs only four to five pounds at birth and clings to its mother for the first few months of life. An infant is able to crawl around at about age six months. Gorillas in captivity can live up to 50 years.

A streak of silver-colored fur is visible on this adult male gorilla. A silverback is the leader of a gorilla group.

Fossey often shared in the Henry family's celebrations. Here, she poses by a piano at Christmastime.

One day, Mary Henry invited Fossey to her home for lunch. Fossey eagerly accepted.

There was always a steady stream of friends and relatives at the Henry residence for the "midday festival," which enchanted Dian. Mary Henry and her family were enthusiastic Roman Catholics. Their friends who were closest to the Church were the most colorful—Father MacPherson, who played bagpipes, and a Frenchman named François, who had been imported by nearby Gethsemane Abbey to teach its Trappist monks how to sing Gregorian chants. People were always dashing in and out of the house; Mary referred to it as the "Henry Hotel."

The festive spirit of the place could be traced to a small, gray-haired woman with big eyes and a rather large nose—Mary's mother, Gaynee Henry. Gaynee was a sincere and kind person. She enjoyed getting to know people, especially those who loved to travel. "A rolling stone gathers polish," she would constantly tell her family. Never judgmental, she would, however, let people know if they weren't doing the right thing, leaving no one in doubt. Her religion was of great comfort to her and had sustained her through the loss of a husband and two children. It became the foundation for happiness in her life. It was Gaynee Henry who attracted Fossey to Roman Catholicism.

Over the course of an evening at the "Henry Hotel," Dian Fossey would be a silent, interested witness to the family recitation of the rosary, a custom that was observed nightly. She eventually grew to share the Henry family's strong attachment to Joe Flanagan, a priest from Boston, Massachusetts. Flanagan was a Jesuit who had once taught philosophy at Boston University and had joined the Order of the Cistercians of the Stricter Observance, commonly known as the Trappist monks. He came to live at Gethsemane Abbey, close to the Henrys' home in Louisville.

Flanagan, known as Father Raymond, was a talkative fellow. When he visited the Henrys, it was difficult for him to follow one of the severe restrictions of the Trappists—a vow of silence. Father Raymond also used mild profanities in his speech. When it was allowed, the Henrys and Fossey would visit Father Raymond at the abbey to give him news of the outside world. Dian Fossey soon became fascinated with this vigorous, athletic, and intellectual priest. He was probably one of the main reasons why she decided to convert from Protestantism to Catholicism. At Dian's baptism—the sacrament that welcomed her into the Catholic Church—Mary White Henry became her godmother, or sponsor. Fossey took the names of Gaynee and Raymond at her confirmation, a Catholic sacrament that recognized her as an adult member of the Church. As long as Fossey remained in Louisville, she worked at being as reverent and faithful to God as the Henrys.

THE ADVENTURE BEGINS

With Gaynee Henry's encouragement, her daughter Mary traveled abroad as much as she could. She visited Europe and the Far East. But it was nothing compared to her visit with the Forrester family in Salisbury, Rhodesia (now Zimbabwe, in Southern Africa). The Forresters—part Austrian, part Irish, and all Catholic—were old friends of Father Raymond and had been frequent visitors to the "Henry Hotel." The Forresters extended invitations to the Henrys to visit anytime they had a mind to go to Africa. They included Dian Fossey, as she was becoming more and more a part of the Henry household.

In 1960, Mary Henry decided to take the Forresters up on their invitation. She flew off to Rhodesia to visit them. When she returned, Fossey was entirely captivated by the animals that Mary had photographed in Africa. Dian dreamed about going to Africa, but it was out of the question for now—it would take thousands of dollars to make the kind of trip she had in mind. She thought of asking her stepfather to finance the trip, but decided that she would rather die before she asked Richard Price for anything. Fossey had to put the dream out of her mind. And for three years, she did just that.

But Fossey's job as an occupational therapist at Kosair was beginning to wear her down. She felt unfulfilled after eight years there. Her job was at a dead end. She knew that she had a lot to give, but in her job, she always had to follow someone else's direction or example. She felt that she was locked into a routine life in Louisville and decided that she had to change it. She determined that she would go on safari in Africa and would go first class all the way. But this would cost $8,000, the equivalent of more than a year and a half of her salary, for a stay of seven weeks. Fossey wanted to hire an experienced guide with a car. That way, she would be free to go anywhere she liked.

Fortunately, Fossey found a bank in Louisville that was willing to lend her the money. The interest rate was high, and she had to pay off the loan within three years, but it was the only solution. Mary Henry also agreed to help Fossey financially. So, with the money in hand, Fossey began to purchase the necessary clothes and boots and insect spray for her trip. She got her travel documents and vaccinations and took lessons in basic Swahili from an African student at the University of Kentucky. Her plan was to fly to Nairobi, Kenya, and stay at the Mount Kenya Safari Club, a first-class place to start from. Once there, she would locate a guide. On the way back, she would visit the Forresters at their farm in Rhodesia.

Going to Africa, the dream that had filled Fossey's life, was about to come true. On September 26, 1963, she left for Nairobi—with 60 pounds of excess baggage. After her arrival at the Safari Club, she arranged for a guide, John Alexander. A 41-year-old Englishman, Alexander had been a national park warden and was a member of the East African Professional Hunters Association. He knew a lot about the behavior of wild animals and appeared to be a perfect choice for Fossey.

Together, they worked out an itinerary that would take them to Tsavo, Kenya, the home of more than 200,000 elephants and many thousands of rhinoceros. They would then go on to Ngorongoro Crater, in Tanzania, a volcano that held in its rim elephants, lions, and hyenas. Just beyond, to the west, Fossey and Alexander planned a stop at Olduvai Gorge in Serengeti National Park, also in Tanzania, where she wanted to meet Dr. Louis Leakey. Leakey had been conducting archaeological research in the area for more than 30 years. Here he had found fossils of early hominids, proving that humans had been around much longer than anyone had thought, and that their roots were in East Africa, not in Asia, as most anthropologists had believed. Alexander knew Leakey well and would introduce him to Fossey.

The field camp at Olduvai looked deserted when Dian Fossey and John Alexander arrived. There were a few drab tin huts and dusty Land Rovers and small trucks in the parking area. All of a sudden, several workers, two dalmatians, and a wildebeest with a monkey on its back appeared.

Louis Leakey conducted many archaeological digs at Olduvai Gorge, Tanzania. The dark rock jutting up from the light ridge contains fossils from prehistoric humans.

Fossey recognized the animals as Louis Leakey's pets. Just as suddenly, Dr. Leakey himself appeared. He greeted them warmly. Grasping Dian Fossey's hands in his, he began to question her about where she had been and where she was planning to go.

She told him that she wanted to meet the mountain gorillas in Uganda's Virunga volcano country (today this region is actually located in two additional countries, Zaire and Rwanda) and that one day she hoped to live and work in Africa. Leakey explained that further studies of the great apes would surely shed light on the evolution and behavior of our ancestors.

Fossey asked if she could take some photographs of Leakey's current dig, where researchers were carefully uncovering the fossilized skull of a giant giraffe. As she was setting up her camera and tripod, she slipped and turned her ankle. John Alexander had to carry her back to camp. Leakey examined the swollen ankle and bandaged it. He then advised her to go see the mountain gorillas despite her twisted ankle. Leakey thought that Fossey was the kind of person who would not let this type of setback change her intended plans.

He was right. Over the next four days, Fossey and Alexander drove west toward Uganda. They finally arrived at Traveller's Rest, a small hotel within hiking distance of mountain-gorilla country. Located on the western slopes of

Louis and Mary Leakey excavate a site at Olduvai Gorge in 1961—two years before Fossey's visit to the area.

the Virungas, a stay at Traveller's Rest was a necessary stop for anyone awaiting news of the gorillas. The proprietor, Walter Baumgärtel, told them that gorillas had been seen not far from his hotel on Mount Mikeno, in Zaire.

Fossey and Alexander crossed into the Zaire section of the Virunga Mountains and, with 11 porters and 2 guides, prepared for the ascent of Mount Mikeno to look for the mountain gorillas. Even though it was tightly bandaged, Fossey's ankle still hurt. During the climb, she started gasping for breath—she was not used to hiking at high altitudes, and she was a heavy smoker. But she continued on, resting often during the six and a half hours it took to climb the 11,000 feet to the top of the mountain, dark with dense vegetation. Finally, they came to an opening where the sunlight shone through the Kabara Meadow.

It was here that Dian Fossey saw mountain gorillas for the first time. Here, she confronted them face to face, not from inside a Land Rover, as she would other animals on a safari. It was a one-on-one experience—there was no place to run in the dense bush of the Virungas, no way to break free of the surrounding vegetation, which the gorillas, unlike humans, can easily walk through. Fossey and her crew had to be prepared not only to watch but to be watched.

Fossey's first contact with the gorillas was their strong smell, which she described as an odor of the barnyard mixed with human sweat. When she first heard their deafening, high-pitched screams, she was scared and almost fled back down the mountain. But then she saw a group of mountain gorillas—about six huge adults with black fur, their leathery faces enlivened by searching brown eyes. The gorillas watched Fossey and her party carefully, trying to see whether or not these strange beings were dangerous.

This brief encounter was to change Dian Fossey's life. She and Alexander left Mount Mikeno the next day, but now she knew that somehow, someday, she would return to Africa to learn more about the Virunga mountain gorillas.

EARLIER RESEARCH ON THE MOUNTAIN GORILLAS

Walter Baumgärtel had purchased his small hotel in Uganda in 1955. Located at the base of the Virunga Mountains, it was the only place in Central Africa where, in the space of one day, the average visitor could enter gorilla country with a good chance of seeing the animals. Baumgärtel loved the mountains that towered near his hotel—and above all the gorillas, who fascinated him. Baumgärtel had also realized that the mountain gorillas had scientific value. Aware of Dr. Louis Leakey's reputation as a scientist, Baumgärtel wrote to him for advice. Leakey sent two young women, who tried to study the gorillas for a year, from 1956 to 1957. The kind of information they gathered, however, was much like that collected in the past—descriptions of nests, food remains found on trails, roars of males when intruded upon. The observations provided only small glimpses of the gorillas' daily social behavior.

In 1957, George Schaller was a young graduate student at the University of Wisconsin. He was working on research into the behavior of birds when a chance remark by one of his zoology professors changed the course of his life. The National Academy of Sciences wanted to begin an expedition to study the behavior of gorillas in Central Africa. Asked if he would be interested in joining the expedition, Schaller impulsively answered that he would.

Gorilla Myths

In 1940, Gargantua the Great was the star attraction of the "Greatest Show on Earth," the Ringling Brothers and Barnum and Bailey Circus. Billed as "The Largest Gorilla Ever Exhibited—The World's Most Terrifying Living Creature," the public flocked to see him.

Gargantua was a male lowland gorilla who had been found in a mountainous district of Central Africa. When he was a year old, the little gorilla was sold to an animal collector, who put him on a ship bound for New York. The collector hoped to get a good price for the good-looking animal.

But sometime during the voyage, and for no reason at all, a sailor squirted nitric acid in the gorilla's face, which permanently damaged his facial muscles and the skin around his eyes. The facial disfigurement greatly lowered his value as a zoo exhibit.

The animal collector sold him at a reduced price to Mrs. Gertrude Linz, a gentle old lady from Brooklyn, New York, whose hobby was making pets of unusual animals. She named her new pet Buddy and hired a trainer to teach him good manners and a few simple tricks. She even had a pair of shoes made especially so that Buddy could walk upright!

Schaller's road to Africa had many twists and turns. Letters had to be written, a sponsor had to be found, and funding had to be obtained. Schaller also had to learn about the gorillas. He read as many books and articles as he could find on the subject.

But most of what he read about the gorillas was fed more by myth and fear than by solid knowledge. Numerous African tales and rumors added to the gorilla myth. The fact

When Buddy was five years old, he weighed more than 400 pounds—certainly too big for a household pet. Mrs. Linz heard that John Ringling North had been looking for a gorilla for his circus. She sold Buddy to North for $10,000. His name was changed to Gargantua the Great (circus people affectionately called him "Gargy"). Gargantua was a fascination to circus-goers of all ages until he died of a lung ailment in 1949. He had been with the circus for 11 years.

Science and entertainment have made gorillas an integral part of modern life through scenes such as that showing movie actress Fay Wray in the clutches of Hollywood's King Kong. In the original movie version of *King Kong*, made in 1933, the gorilla was a screen illusion. He was made to be frightening and believable by adventurous movie pioneer Marian C. Cooper and special-effects wizard Willis O'Brien. In order to create an artificial ten-story-tall gorilla, the pair created an 18-inch-tall model of a gorilla. When the gorilla model was in position, one film frame was exposed. Each time the model was moved, another frame was exposed. It actually took ten hours to expose just 30 seconds of film. For closeups, a huge gorilla hand, eight feet high, was constructed. Fay Wray performed her scenes and was photographed in the hand.

was, much of the world knew little about Africa, and even less about the great apes, until the late 1950s. The gorilla was usually described as a ferocious, bloodthirsty, and treacherous animal. The photographs would show a gorilla shot through the head, propped against a tree, a hunter squatting next to the huge body. Or a photograph might show an adventurer, holding onto his camera, crashing through the tall vegetation, followed by many porters.

Schaller came to the conclusion that there was very little concrete information about the gorillas other than the basic facts about their size and shape. Little was known about their actual behavior. How do gorillas live in the wild? Do they live in small units or large groups? How many males and females are there in each group? What do groups do when they meet? How far do they travel every day? How long are babies dependent on their mothers? All these questions remained unanswered. Schaller wondered, though, if gorillas could actually be studied—it would require many uninterrupted hours of observing the animals in the wild.

Finally, in 1959, after months of meetings and discussions, Schaller left for Africa to begin a pioneering study of the rare mountain gorillas in Uganda and Belgian Congo. (The Belgian Congo became independent in 1960, and was known thereafter as Zaire.) The purpose of the study was to learn the distribution of the mountain gorilla, the various types of vegetation that the gorilla encounters over the whole of its range, and the similarities and differences in food and nesting habits and other behavior. He eventually found a location where gorillas could be studied, and he observed for about a year the behavior of a single population of gorillas. Schaller studied 200 gorillas in ten groups. But in September 1960, there was political unrest in the region and he had to bring his study to an end.

He reported his experiences for the general public in two books, *The Mountain Gorilla* and *The Year of the Gorilla*. Thanks to George Schaller, the huge, gentle ape began to shed its reputation as a terrifying monster bent on the destruction of everyone in its path.

How did the mountain gorilla earn such a bad reputation in the first place?

"Half Man-Half Beast"

In 470 B.C., an expedition of colonists left Carthage in a fleet of ships. On the coast of West Africa, they encountered hairy, stone-throwing creatures that they called *Gorillai*. Two thousand years passed before European explorers added more information. In 1774, a British sea captain reported a "wonderful and frightful production of nature...7 to 9 feet high...thick in proportion and amazingly strong...."

In 1846, American missionary Thomas S. Savage found a gorilla skull beside the Gabon River in West Africa. He sent it to two scientists, along with hair-raising descriptions: "They are exceedingly ferocious and always offensive in their habits...it is said that when the male is first seen he gives a terrific yell that resounds far and wide through the forest...."

Ten years later, an American journalist traveled to West Africa. He became the first person to "bag," or catch, a gorilla. Paul Belloni du Chaillu wrote about his adventure in 1861. The book was an immediate success, but his dramatic descriptions portrayed the gorilla as "some hellish dream creature...half man–half beast"—an impression that persisted into the twentieth century.

At the turn of the century, the focus on the gorilla shifted from West Africa to the mountainous regions of eastern Belgian Congo and western Uganda. German hunter Oscar Von Beringe, an official of the Tanganyika Railway, had come to Africa to do some mountain climbing in 1903. He was the first to shoot a mountain gorilla, then the least known of the great apes. The carcass was examined by a German taxonomist (someone who determines scientific classifications). He named the separate subspecies *Gorilla*

Paul Belloni du Chaillu's book left readers with the impression that gorillas were diabolic creatures.

gorilla beringei, after Von Beringe. Then, in the early 1920s, American naturalist Carl Akeley led an expedition to the Belgian Congo side of the Virunga Mountains to hunt specimens for the American Museum of Natural History in New York City. While there, he shot five gorillas; their stuffed bodies can be seen today in the African Room of the museum. But he was so upset about what he had done that he urged Belgian king Albert to set aside a sanctuary for the gorillas, where they could live in peace and be studied by scientists. In 1922, the Belgian Congo part of the Virungas was set aside as a national park to protect gorillas.

In 1926, Akeley returned to Africa, but he fell ill while on safari and died. His wish was to be buried in Kabara Meadow, between Mount Karisimbi and Mount Mikeno on the Belgian Congo side of the Virungas.

When Dian Fossey first visited Kabara Meadow in 1963, she thought it was the most beautiful place on Earth. She promised herself that one day she would return there. Albert National Park, named after the Belgian king, was established in 1925. In 1929, it was enlarged to include the entire chain of the Virunga Mountains.

LOVE AT FIRST SIGHT

After having said goodbye to John Alexander, Dian Fossey left East Africa and headed for Salisbury, the capital of Rhodesia, to visit the Forrester family. Salisbury was a lot like Louisville, Kentucky—too large to be intimate, and too small to be impersonal. At the Forresters' farm, Dian felt at home, just like at the "Henry Hotel." The visit proved to be a perfect ending to her African adventure, because it was there that she met Alexie Forrester.

Peg and Franz Forrester had raised their three sons—Michael, Alexie, and Robert ("Pookie")—as pioneers in this frontier country. They were exuberant and outgoing. They were also among the last remnants of an era of aristocratic British colonialism in Africa. (In 1965, Rhodesia became independent of Great Britain. In 1980, it was renamed Zimbabwe. Salisbury was renamed Harare.)

Soon after Fossey's arrival, Peg Forrester introduced her to Alexie. (Back in Louisville, Father Raymond had shown Fossey Alexie's photograph; Dian had commented, "That's my boy!") Alexie, six feet six inches tall, was almost a head taller than Dian and seven years younger. He had a round face and strawberry-blond hair. Alexie ran the family farm, overseeing the work of 200 field hands. Dian and Alexie liked each other immediately. They agreed to meet again the following year in the United States, where Alexie planned to enter Notre Dame University, in South Bend, Indiana.

Captivated by Africa, Dian Fossey returned to Louisville. She drifted back into the placid Louisville routine. She continued to remain close to the Henrys, and her work at Kosair went on as usual. She attended Catholic mass daily and looked after her stray dogs. In her spare time, she began writing magazine articles about her grand African adventure. She stopped eating lunch to save money and used half her salary to pay back the loan that she had taken out for her trip to Africa.

Alexie Forrester visited Dian at Thanksgiving of 1964. By then, it was obvious to everyone that they had fallen in love. They became engaged to be married the following year. But Alexie was determined to graduate from Notre Dame University, and Dian was just as eager to see him finish his studies. Dian's mother, Kitty, and her stepfather, Richard, flew to Louisville later that year to meet the Forresters at the "Henry Hotel." Then the Forresters flew to California to stay with the Prices. Kitty Price was thrilled: Her daughter was going to marry an aristocrat.

During this exciting period, Dian was still struggling financially, trying to pay off the bank loan. She moved from the Washhouse to an even more remote farmhouse with no heat or running water. She still had her privacy and her dogs, but little else.

THE SECOND MEETING

Then Dr. Louis Leakey came to Louisville on his 1966 lecture tour, and everything changed. Would Leakey recognize her after three years? Dian hoped so; she wanted badly to return to Africa, and she knew that he was the only one who could help her. She waited in the long line after the lecture was over, and her turn to talk to Leakey finally came. "Miss Fossey, isn't it?" He did recognize her! "And how is your ankle? Did it heal properly?" he asked. Dian was astonished and flattered that Leakey had remembered the clumsy tourist of three years ago.

When they met again the following morning, Leakey told Fossey that 22 applicants had been interviewed for gorilla fieldwork study, but none had satisfied him. Leakey was impressed by Fossey's strong desire to return to Africa to work with gorillas, but he could not hire her until he found the necessary funding. He thus put her on hold and returned to Nairobi. It was at this point that Fossey quit her job at Korsair and prepared to go back to Africa.

Dian awaited word from Leakey in California, at her parents' home in Atherton. Although she was in touch with Leakey, who told her his intention was for her to go to Africa, the hot summer of 1966 passed without any further information from Dr. Leakey. Living with her less-than-enthusiastic mother and stepfather—who thought she was crazy to go to Africa—was uncomfortable, especially after so many years being on her own. But Fossey passed the time productively, attending a primatology (study of primates) class at Stanford University in Palo Alto, close to where she was staying.

She began to worry that the gorilla project would never get off the ground. In September, Fossey wrote Leakey, who replied that he had submitted grant proposals to the National Geographic Society. In desperation, she again wrote to Leakey in October to tell him that she had quit her job of 11 years, cutting off her only source of income. Was she going to Africa or not? She wanted to know. At last, on November 3, Leakey cabled that the Wilkie Brothers Foundation, which had also backed Jane Goodall's chimpanzee studies in Tanzania, had come through with a $3,000 grant, enough to establish a gorilla project. The Wilkies

Jane Goodall has spent 35 years studying chimpanzees in the wild. Today, she travels around the world promoting conservation and protection of endangered animals.

agreed with Leakey that, by studying humans' closest living relatives, the great apes, new information could be found about how our ancestors might have behaved. A few weeks later, the National Geographic Society also agreed to help fund the project.

Dian was on her way. Her mother and stepfather, however, tried again and again to talk her out of going. They could not understand her strong desire to undertake such an unconventional life. Father Raymond, though, looked upon the African research project as a "gift from God." He recognized that Dian Fossey was different from most people, that she yearned for some truly tremendous accomplishment. The gorilla project was a special project for a special person.

Fossey clung fiercely to her decision. She packed her typewriter, four cameras, a tripod, lenses, many rolls of film, office supplies, and paper—enough to equip a small office—and a three-year supply of heavy outerwear, including jeans, parkas, and army surplus ponchos. The course of her life was about to change.

On Monday, December 19, 1966, Dian Fossey flew from the United States to East Africa. It would be her home for the next 18 years.

FROM
KENTUCKY
TO ZAIRE

Dian Fossey did not seem a likely candidate for a serious field researcher. Her health was not good. She had bad lungs. She wheezed. Physically, she was fragile.

She was also naive. While it is true that she loved dogs and horses, they were domestic animals, nothing like the wild mountain gorillas. She knew little of the local African languages, although she had studied some Swahili. She could not speak French, which was spoken in the region around Kabara Meadow and Albert National Park as well as west of the Virunga Mountains. She knew nothing about living in a rain forest, walking in constant mud up steep slopes and down hidden ravines through endless fog and rain mixed with hailstones. She would have to endure wet clothes and wet tents. She had never lived in a tent.

Jane Goodall had at least worked in Dr. Louis Leakey's office and had studied animal behavior for a year after that before she left for the wilderness of Tanzania, taking her mother with her. In contrast, Dian Fossey's experience with Africa was as just a tourist. She lacked many of the scientific skills needed for research. Yet, though she was not a trained scientist, Dian Fossey had the energy and zeal needed for the demands of the job. And she never gave up. Leakey continued to encourage her. He admired her ambition and determination. He instinctively knew that she would prove to be an excellent primate researcher.

The Hutu, Tutsi, and Batwa tribes, peoples who had lived in the Virungas for more than 400 years, were entirely foreign to Dian Fossey. The Belgians had been chased out of Congo by rebels who hated all whites and allied themselves with Chinese Communists. In one part of the eastern Belgian Congo, the rebels had murdered 2,000 to 4,000 Africans and had held 1,000 Belgians and Americans hostage. Most whites had fled the area. Dian Fossey had never worked anywhere outside the United States. Yet she ventured forth alone and seemingly unafraid, proceeding on the long journey from Kentucky to Zaire.

SETTING UP CAMP

Fossey arrived in Nairobi, Kenya, with a cold—coughing, sniffing, and feverish. After a few days, however, she felt much better.

Leakey now insisted that she have the proper equipment for her trip to Kabara Meadow. With money from the Wilkie Brothers study grant, Leakey purchased a used Land Rover for Dian. He test-drove the vehicle himself to break it in. Fossey quickly named it "Lily," but it took her some time to get the hang of driving it. When she failed to double-clutch or she stalled in a warthog hole, one of Fossey's African assistants accompanying her would yell in frustration in Swahili (in order to understand what was said, she had to look up the words in her dictionary).

Leakey had arranged for nature photographer and film-maker Alan Root to take Fossey to Kabara Meadow, where he would help her set up camp. With his wife Joan, he wrote and produced films on subjects like the social life of termites and the evolution of the rain forest. The cast of their films included animals, plants, rocks, fire, and weather—all chosen for their particular talents. Alan Root was an animal lover and always carried a camera instead of a gun. Root would be Dian's "first guide to survival."

Things began to move fast. Fossey went shopping for food. Root wanted her to take seasonings and herbs and canned foods, but she picked her favorites: orange squash, cakes, and starches. Lily was finally packed, and, with Alan Root in his Land Rover just ahead, Fossey finally started on the 700-mile-trip from Nairobi to Kabara Meadow, where she hoped to base her studies. They drove down deteriorating roads filled with deep mud ruts, traveling mostly by day, as night driving proved too risky.

Something went wrong with the steering of Fossey's Land Rover. She complained to Root that there was a problem with it. Then the right front wheel fell off. Root fixed it but said the steering problem was her imagination. At the Ugandan border, they were delayed because Fossey had no car registration. And Root had forgotten his visa, a travel document needed to enter the country. After joking with the border guards and giving them some of Root's gorilla photographs, they were allowed to enter Uganda. When they finally reached Rumangabo, the outlying post for the military in the Kivu Province of Zaire, Root located Sanweckwe, a trustworthy tracker who had worked with George Schaller. Root made arrangements to have Sanweckwe work a two-week cycle along with a cook and a woodsman. At Kibumba, a tiny village at the base of Mount Mikeno, Root hired 42 porters to get Fossey's gear up the mountain and to help her set up camp, dig a latrine, and install a drainage system.

On January 15, 1967, Alan Root left to return to Nairobi. Fossey now felt very alone. The only thing that felt familiar was a shortwave radio that Louis Leakey had given her; at least she could hear the BBC radio broadcast in English. The 7-by 9-foot tent set up on the edge of the Kabara Meadow was to be used for sleeping and working. Fossey avoided the two Africans who remained as camp staff—she could not understand a word they said.

The next morning, on her 35th birthday, Fossey came upon a male gorilla resting on a heavy tree trunk extending over the edge of a small pond. She would learn later that gorillas usually avoid water, and she would never again see such a sight. But she regarded this as a favorable introduction to the object of her study. She wrote Leakey she would stay for at least two years, even if it killed her! This was longer than Schaller had stayed.

Dian Fossey quickly became adapted to her new home. Sanweckwe presented her with a chicken and a rooster, which she promptly named Lucy and Dezi, after the television stars Lucille Ball and Desi Arnaz. Other companions included two Egyptian geese, which Fossey named

Dian feeds one of the two ravens she befriended
while living in the Kabara Meadow camp.

Smith-Corona and Olivetti, after the typewriter brands, and
two ravens, who patrolled the Kabara Meadow. Most of the
time, it rained or was foggy. There were especially heavy
downpours in March and April, with hailstones the size of
golf balls.

In her first two weeks of research, Fossey piled up 23
hours, 17 minutes of observation from nine contacts with
two gorilla groups. On February 24, 1967, she recorded two

new births. She had compiled 200 typed pages of field notes. Leakey considered her work first-rate.

Fossey sent monthly field reports to Leakey, who said that he was pleased with her progress. Funding—from the New York Zoological Society, African Wildlife Leadership Foundation, Royal Little (a wealthy conservationist), and National Geographic Society—eventually totaled more than $16,000. The National Geographic Society encouraged her to write, lecture, and make personal appearances; she learned that Alan Root would return to photograph her at work. The photos would accompany her articles about her research. At last, Dian Fossey was going to *be* somebody.

Fossey was frightened sometimes, and lonely. Sanweckwe became her chief support, even though they could not communicate well. He was indispensable to Fossey. From him, she learned how to handle herself in her new environment. She raised his salary and gave him rubber boots and new clothes. Fossey soon entrusted her life to him, even though there were many things about Sanweckwe that she could not understand. However, she sensed that he both understood and respected the gorillas. And, as the long months wore on, this was of great importance to her.

A Hatred of Poachers

One day, after eight hours in the bush studying the gorillas, Dian arrived at the meadow in pouring rain only to find the Africans literally covered in blood. Poachers (people who illegally kill animals) had killed a buffalo and its calf, and the carcasses were being shared all around. To Fossey, it looked barbaric. When the Africans offered her what they considered delicacies—buffalo intestines and brains—all she wanted to do was throw up.

Fossey knew that buffalos were an endangered species and that killing them was illegal, but she considered feasting on their remains just as bad. The Africans, however, felt differently: The buffalos were dead, and they were hungry, so why not use the meat?

The episode marked the beginning of a long—and perhaps fateful—battle that Dian Fossey was to wage against poachers in Africa. To her, poachers were outlaws.

WAR BREAKS OUT

In July 1967, civil war broke out in Rwanda. The situation became extremely dangerous. The border between Uganda and Zaire suddenly closed, and a state of national emergency was declared. The government announced that any aircraft violating its air space would be shot down. Fossey, still dangerously uninformed about Africa and its politics, suddenly found herself face to face with the enemy.

On July 9, Fossey's camp was surrounded by armed soldiers, who informed her that there was a rebellion going on in Kivu Province in Zaire and that she should be evacuated for her own safety. She was escorted down the mountain the next morning and then held in Rumangabo, where she was detained by the soldiers for 16 days in a room in a large farmhouse. She passed the days studying French and reviewing her field notes. With chances for her release lessening by the hour, Fossey decided to escape. She persuaded the soldiers to drive her into Kisoro to pick up her Land Rover where she told them she had left all her money.

She drove her Land Rover across the border post at Bunagana. It was packed with her field notes, a pistol in a tissue box, her typewriter, and her camera. At the border post, suspicious and jumpy soldiers ordered Fossey to surrender. She persuaded them that it was to everyone's advantage if she went to Uganda to get her money. She had to surrender her passport, and, with a guard accompanying her, she headed for Traveller's Rest to stay with Walter Baumgärtel. When she arrived, she fled from the guard, and ran to a room in the back of the inn. Baumgärtel managed to get the guard to leave without Fossey.

The word had been relayed that Fossey would be shot on sight by soldiers if she tried to return to Zaire. She somehow managed to get back to Nairobi to see Dr. Leakey. She would need new visas and assistance in returning to Kabara Meadow to study the gorillas.

With Leakey's intervention, Fossey flew back to the Rwandan side of the Virungas within two weeks. There were still more gorillas to locate and mountains to climb.

KARISOKE

Fossey was sure that gorillas lived around Mount Visoke and Mount Karisimbi in Rwanda. (These mountains also share borders with Zaire.) She would go there and start over, she decided. Baumgärtel said that, when she got there, the person to look up was his friend Alyette de Munck, a Belgian woman who had grown up in Zaire's Kivu Province. De Munck was a self-taught naturalist endowed with common-sense knowledge of the country and its traditions. She had photographed erupting volcanoes in the Virungas

Due to political turmoil in the region, Fossey was forced to move her research from the Kabara Meadow to a new camp. Here, she watches porters carry her belongings into the Rwandan mountains.

and had collected poisonous snakes for Leakey's Corydon Museum in Nairobi. She would surely know where the gorillas were in Rwanda!

Fossey loaded her Land Rover and drove along the single paved road to Rwanda. Several hours later, she arrived at de Munck's house. There, she learned that de Munck's son and nephew had been arrested and killed by the Congolese military when their car had accidentally taken a wrong turn. They had been mistaken for mercenaries—soldiers-for-hire.

Fossey did what she could to comfort de Munck. She stayed with her while investigating a suitable location for her gorilla research. On the tenth day of her search, she found a region of deep ravines surrounded by steep ridges between Mount Karisimbi and Mount Visoke, a habitat that appeared to be just right for gorillas. She knew at once that this is where she would set up camp. At precisely 4:30 in the afternoon on September 24, 1967, Fossey founded the Karisoke Research Center. The word *Karisoke* was a combination of Mount *Kari*simbi and Mount Vi*soke*.

The prospect of finding gorillas began to cheer Fossey. She was up and running; Karisoke now became her home. Fossey had not contacted anyone in the United States for months. She could hardly believe that only one year earlier, she had been making plans to marry Alexie Forrester. Now that everything had changed, she had forgotten those plans. She felt that she had more important things to do. The mountain gorillas had become the focus of her life.

BREAKTHROUGH

For 12 years, Louis Leakey had been looking for the right person to study mountain gorillas. Fossey had surpassed even what he had expected of her. She had already exceeded Schaller's 466 hours of gorilla observation; in less than a year, she had accrued 485 hours. She had located and identified four new groups of gorillas. And every hour that she spent with the gorillas provided its own satisfaction.

Probably her most rewarding experience occurred less than a year after the Karisoke research began. The youngest male in his group, Peanuts, was feeding about 15 feet away from Fossey when he suddenly stopped and stared directly at her. Then he sighed deeply and slowly resumed eating.

An inactive Visoke volcano's crater is filled with a pool of water. The heavy foliage around the crater and in the region serves as the habitat for the mountain gorilla.

She cabled Leakey at once: "I've finally been accepted by a gorilla."

Two years after they exchanged glances, Peanuts left his feeding group and walked toward Fossey. Slowly, she left the moss-cushioned hagenia tree where she had been sitting and pretended to munch on vegetation. In that way, she was reassuring Peanuts that she did not want to harm him.

Peanuts looked at Fossey with his bright eyes. He began to strut and swagger. Suddenly, he came to sit down by her side and watch her "eat." Fossey scratched her head.

Peanuts scratched his. Fossey lay back in the grass and slowly extended her hand, palm upward, and rested it on the leaves. Peanuts then stood up, and he extended his hand to touch his fingers against hers for an instant. Seemingly thrilled at his daring, Peanuts pounded his chest before leaving to rejoin his group.

The spot where this first gorilla-to-human physical contact took place became known as Fasi Ya Mkoni, "The Place of the Hands." Fossey considered this experience to be among the most memorable contacts of her long life among the mountain gorillas.

Eventually Peanuts shifted his range out of the Karisoke study area. A year passed with only an occasional sighting or trail sign to confirm his whereabouts. Then, in March 1977, Peanuts was found. By then, he was 15 years old and mature.

By 1972, there were 96 gorillas in the study area. They lived in eight family groups. Fossey spent most of her time with Group 4. By this time, she had practically become a member of their family. Group 4 was made up of 14 gorillas led by a silverback that Fossey named Whinny, because his cries sounded like a horse. He had bad lungs, which accounted for the whinny noise. Whinny died at 30 years of age, young for a gorilla.

Two silverbacks in Group 4 were named Amok and Uncle Bert (the latter named after Fossey's favorite uncle). They were often found playing with the group's youngsters. Over the years, Fossey watched the group change through births and deaths, recording and interpreting their activities. She was often surrounded by the youngsters in Group 4, who came to treat her like one of their own. On many occasions, note taking would be abandoned as Fossey just played with

From Kentucky to Zaire

The Fossey Method: Studying the Mountain Gorilla

Dian Fossey became well acquainted with many of the gorillas over the years, and they with her. Gorillas roam the misty wooded mountain slopes of the Virunga range in groups. Several groups began to accept Fossey as a member. She was able to come within a few feet of them. Some had come closer to her, picking up her camera strap and even examining the buckle on her knapsack.

She came to know the gorillas as individuals with their own unique personalities. Fossey named them for identification purposes. She was not satisfied to just sit and observe; instead, she tried to gain their confidence by acting like them. She imitated their feeding and grooming behavior. She copied their voices, even making their deep belching noises! Unscientific methods, maybe, but they worked.

In her first year at Karisoke, Fossey concentrated her observations on four main groups, totaling 51 individuals, living within the 9 1/2-square-mile study area around the camp. The groups had between five and 19 members, the average being 13. Identified by number according to the order contacted, these were Groups 4, 5, 8, and 9. Fossey tried to distribute observation hours evenly among these four main study groups.

Sometimes Dian observed a group from a tree. Sometimes Peanuts, Geezer, and Samson, three young males, would climb up to join her to investigate her boots, clothes, and camera equipment.

A popular gorilla game is sliding—infants practice on the mother's body, then graduate to tree trunks. The favorite playtime seems to be a sunny morning or after an afternoon rest period.

Three silverbacks in Group 5—Brahms, Bartok, and Beethoven—showed Fossey just how far they would go to protect their young. One day, an infant, Icarus, was trying out an acrobatic routine in a tree when the tree came crashing down. Icarus, none the worse for wear, calmly climbed another tree. Brahms, Bartok, and Beethoven charged toward Fossey, apparently thinking she was responsible. Then another infant climbed the same broken sapling and began a series of spins, twirls, and chest pats. The eyes of the silverbacks

Fossey was able to gain the trust of some of the gorillas she observed.

darted back and forth between the infant and Fossey. When their glances met, she felt their disapproval.

But it was Icarus who broke the uneasiness. He climbed to the other infant's tree and began a game of tag, which led both animals back to the group. Brahms gave a tension-releasing chest beat, and Bartok and Beethoven followed suit. The crisis had passed.

A young female gorilla named Puck, gently strokes Fossey's hair. Fossey had to be accepted by Puck's parents before she could become friendly with the gorilla.

the gorillas. She dozed with them in the sun. She tickled the infants—"Just too thrilling for words," she exclaimed.

Fossey became especially attached to a bright-eyed young male, an inquisitive ball of black fluff. His twisted middle finger was prominent—it appeared to have been broken—so Fossey named him Digit. Digit was about five years old at their first encounter in September 1967. Fossey continued to

Fossey eagerly contacted Group 5 and was able to come as close as 20 feet during her first year of fieldwork at Karisoke. On contact, she crawled up to Group 5 carrying a heavy tape recorder. About 20 feet below the gorillas, who were feeding above, she made her presence known, set up the microphone in a nearby tree, and stabilized the tape recorder on the ground.

A number of curious young gorillas climbed into the trees above her to stare at the strange equipment. They became wilder and noisier. The silverbacks began to charge within ten feet of Dian. The screaming became so intense that the modulation meter on the recorder went berserk. Dian whispered to herself, "I'll never get out of this alive!" But the group eventually climbed out of sight. She turned off the recorder and returned to her cabin. Fossey had discovered that gorillas could identify one another by voice, even over great distances.

On other days, Fossey would crawl to the edge of a ridge and lay hidden in the brush to observe the animals with her binoculars. The observation of a silverback with his offspring showed the gentleness of the adult male gorilla—dispelling all the myths about King Kong.

One afternoon following a successful three-hour contact, Fossey put down her notebook filled with that day's behavioral observations. Suddenly, a young male gorilla ran forward and snatched the notebook. Fossey started to crawl after him, but before she could reach him, he began to tear out page after page of her carefully recorded data. He chewed each page to a pulp.

observe Digit for the next four years. By the time he was nine, Digit was too old to play with his younger siblings but too young to associate with Group 4's older females.

One cold and rainy day, Fossey found Digit about 30 feet away from the rest of the group. She did not want to interfere with his show of independence, so she decided to leave him alone. Fossey settled herself several yards away. A few

Digit and Fossey shared a strong gorilla-human bond. Here she sits with him in May 1977—he is about 15 years old.

minutes passed. All of a sudden, she felt an arm around her shoulders. Fossey looked up into Digit's warm, gentle brown eyes. Then he patted her on the head and settled down by her side.

Digit became strongly attracted to humans. He showed that he could tell the difference between men and women: He would charge playfully at men but would act coy around women. He became fascinated by human artifacts such as notebooks, gloves, and camera equipment, always examining, smelling, and handling everything gently. Fossey found him completely lovable.

A Friend to Animals

Gorillas weren't Fossey's only animal friends. Cindy, Fossey's most beloved pet, was a big brown boxer that came to her as a puppy—a gift from friends—and became the companion that she had been denied throughout her childhood. Along with other animals, she also adopted a monkey named Kima. Louis Leakey, who had once owned a monkey, warned Fossey that the animal would be a handful, but Fossey adopted the two-year-old female anyway. Kima was destructive and wreaked havoc at the camp. Bamboo shoots, fruits, and vegetables were not enough to satisfy Kima. She developed a passion for human food, especially beer. No one's dinner was safe.

Kima roamed the camp and terrified visitors with her loud screeching and biting. She often bit Fossey's hands when brought indoors against her will. All night or in bad weather, Kima had the run of Fossey's cabin.

Fossey never could tolerate anyone who abused animals. Once, when she was driving through a crowded, dusty African village, she saw a man beating his dog. She stopped the car and ran to the dog's rescue. The dog beater fled. Dian lifted the animal into the back of her car and took it back to Karisoke to be nursed back to health. Eventually, the animal was returned to its owner, who was given instructions for the dog's care and a warning that if Fossey found the animal mistreated again, she would remove it for good.

Fossey's animal companions at the Karisoke research camp included Cindy the dog and Kima the monkey.

FOSSEY'S CAUSE ATTRACTS WORLDWIDE ATTENTION

In an attempt to attract visitors to the Volcano National Park, the Rwandan Tourist Office in Kigali asked Fossey for a photograph of a gorilla to use as a poster advertisement. She selected a color photo that she had taken of Digit feeding on a piece of wood in 1972, when he was about ten. The poster read, "Come to meet him in Rwanda." Digit was about to become world-famous.

As Digit matured, he had much less interest in humans. He had become head of his group and thus had a role as a potential breeder and guard. There were constant threats to the gorillas. At that time, most gorillas were wild and afraid of humans. They were hard to approach. The only people they had had contact with were poachers, most of whom were Batwa. Batwa poachers pursued antelope with their spears, often running right past Fossey's cabin. Some of the Volcano National Park guards allowed the poachers to roam freely.

The Batwa are hunter-gatherers alert to the life of the forest. They consider farming dull and demeaning work. They like to lay snares, or traps, for antelope—a forest antelope would put one foot in a snare and quickly be thrown up in the air.

As the Rwandan population grew, the government had to expand the amount of land available for farming. In 1969, some 22,000 acres had been taken away from the park. As a result, the gorilla habitat shrank to only 30,000 acres, and the gorillas encountered poachers more often. Sometimes a gorilla would get a hand or foot caught in a snare. It broke Fossey's heart to see a gorilla limping with an infected foot with a wire noose in it. She came to view the Batwa as the main threat to the mountain gorillas.

Fossey was determined to fight back. She burned poacher's camps, threw away their food, and cut their snares. She once kidnapped the son of a well-known poacher to use him as a bargaining chip. In turn, the poachers struck back, using local magic spells to frighten her. They believed that only powerful magic could protect her from the gorillas, which they feared deeply. In return, to scare off poachers, Fossey and her staff would put on Halloween masks and throw

Fossey works outside of her cabin at the Karisoke Research Center. She would bury Digit in front of her home.

firecrackers on poacher raids. Fossey would go to Kigali to stock up on scary masks and plastic worms.

Fossey's campaign against poachers came to a turning point in December 1977. As trackers were dismantling a trap line that month, they came across Digit. His head and hands had been cut off. He had taken five mortal spear wounds while holding off six poachers and their dogs, in order to let his gorilla family members flee to safety. Digit managed to kill one of the poachers' dogs before he died.

Dian Fossey was shattered. "From that moment on," she later said, "I came to live within an insulated part of myself."

Digit's body was carried back to camp and buried in front of Fossey's cabin. But she refused to bury his memory, feeling that there was much to be gained by telling the world about Digit's death.

Anchorman Walter Cronkite announced Digit's death on the "CBS Evening News," and *The New York Times* reported it. Fossey hoped that public outcry over this murder might pressure Rwandan government officials to put poachers in jail for a long time. Fossey launched a fund in Digit's name to help support the active protection of gorillas. The donations would be used to expand poacher controls in the park.

Fossey allowed herself to become something of a celebrity so that worldwide attention would be focused on keeping the remaining gorillas alive. By this point, she had all but abandoned scientific research to devote her time to fighting the poachers. The Rwandans, however, had other plans. They wanted to take over Karisoke and make it into a tourist attraction. Dian Fossey was becoming a problem to them, and so, in 1978, there was a concentrated effort to get her out of Rwanda.

NYIRAMACHABELLI! NYIRAMACHABELLI!

"THE WOMAN WHO LIVES ALONE ON THE MOUNTAIN"

Alexie Forrester was determined to bring Dian Fossey back to America as his wife. In October 1967, after a day of gorilla tracking, Dian returned to her cabin at Karisoke to find Alexie waiting for her. He had bribed the soldiers guarding the Rwandan border with cigarettes and a bottle of wine just to get to Karisoke.

Alexie, a Rhodesian, knew Africa well. He thought that most Americans do not have much sensitivity about living outside their own country. He knew that Dian didn't—she felt that "she could go around insisting on her rights" in Africa. As a white woman living on a mountain, she was particularly vulnerable.

After a day of research, Fossey would spend the evening typing
her field notes while her observations were still fresh in her mind.

During the five days that Alexie stayed with Dian, he tried to convince her to leave Africa and marry him. But Forrester had been out of her picture for a long time. About a year earlier, Fossey, in her application for a grant from the National Geographic Society, had indicated her intention to devote at least two years to studying mountain gorillas. She had already made 300 gorilla sightings, she told Alexie, watching them by day and typing her notes by night. Nothing had stood in her way up to now and nothing would now. And so Alexie Forrester walked away from Dian Fossey.

But before he left, he told her if she stayed on the mountain, her throat would be cut by somebody by the end of the year. He said that it was crazy to live alone on a mountain, "harassing a bunch of poachers and expecting to stay alive." It took a lot longer than a year—but, sadly, Alexie's projection proved to be right.

HER TRUE HOME

Karisoke had become Fossey's true home. She had not contacted anyone in the States for months. Her friends in Louisville, Kentucky, were worried about her, but Gaynee Henry continued to keep up Fossey's medical insurance and have her films processed. By the end of 1967, Father Raymond had become so concerned that he wrote Dr. Leakey asking for some word. The Prices in California were so displeased with Dian that she was not going to marry Alexie that they stopped writing to her altogether.

Dr. Leakey became involved in her family matters. He wrote the Prices, assuring them that Dian would achieve an outstanding place in the scientific world and that she would

Fossey examines gorilla bones in her cabin at Karisoke.

have fame and success equal to that of Jane Goodall, who was working with chimpanzees in Tanzania.

Yet Dr. Leakey was never free of worry for Dian's safety. In one of her first letters to him from Rwanda, she told him that her cook, Phocas, whom she had brought with her from Zaire, had threatened to take her life. Another time, when she fired a staffer for smoking marijuana, he had returned to camp to attack her and Fossey had fired a bullet over his head. One of her guides said that the Congolese had offered a reward for her capture and that there were soldiers looking for her. Leakey was very alarmed. He cabled, "…You must take no unnecessary risks, if think necessary abandon project."

But Fossey persisted. She stayed at the camp in the rain forest, where only five days of sunlight penetrated the forest in the winter months. One's feet could actually grow mold. Fossey's teeth were bothering her, and she took codeine, which helped her sleep. When her gold inlays fell out, she collected them for the next visit to the dentist to save money. After 16 months on the mountain, however, Fossey did need a break. She now began to think seriously about getting an advanced scientific degree.

It had always bothered her that she was not academically qualified to study mountain gorillas. Dr. Leakey had become concerned, too, and he urged Fossey to enroll at Cambridge University in England—then the most advanced center for the study of wild-animal behavior—to study for her doctoral degree.

Finally, in 1971, she entered Darwin College at Cambridge to study under Leakey's friend and Jane Goodall's professor, Robert Hinde, the person responsible for making Cambridge one of the world's most important centers for primate studies. Hinde became Fossey's academic supervisor and replaced Leakey as her scientific mentor, or primary teacher.

Hinde was the head of graduate studies in animal behavior. A Royal Air Force pilot in World War II, he had trained in southern Rhodesia. With his austere appearance, rigorous standards, and precise reasoning, he could be intimidating. Hinde was a former ornithologist, a specialist in the study of birds, who had turned to the study of apes and research into mother/child relationships.

The Cambridge Years

At the outset, Fossey was charmed by Cambridge when she began her first three-month term there. But later on she began to have second thoughts about the place. She hated the dark, gray winter mornings in England. There were too many rules to follow at the university, and she missed the gorillas dreadfully. She felt confined and often thought that she was wasting her time. But she knew that to advance in a scientific field and to get financial support and people to work on various projects, a doctoral degree was a necessity. Without a Ph.D., she would be limited in what she could do.

For the next few years, Fossey traveled back and forth between Cambridge and Karisoke. She faced the problem of finding someone who was capable of minding the camp and the gorillas in her absence, but there was no shortage of candidates. A story about her and the gorillas had made the cover of *National Geographic* in January 1970, and her name was becoming well known. She received requests from all sorts of people wanting to come to Karisoke to see and study the gorillas.

Fossey set about arranging a program to develop Karisoke into a first-class research station. In 1969, she had started census work, counting gorillas and evaluating group ranges in the Virunga Mountains. Eventually, with the assistance of students, the scope of research was expanded on an almost yearly basis. Over the next 11 years, about 21 census workers would come to Karisoke to train. The work was quite rugged, and many would return home after very short stays.

Fossey hired two researchers to conduct a census of the gorillas. She encouraged a Cambridge psychiatrist to make comparative studies of gorilla and human skulls. She also found a scientist to make sketches of the gorillas, and she had the help of two zoology students who were willing to do anything just for the privilege of working with her.

When she was in England, Fossey longed for her gorillas, she missed them so much. In her absence, Karisoke was left in the charge of a British zoologist who was looking for doctorate-level research work. Alan Goodall (no relation to Jane) had come recommended by Dr. Hinde. Fossey interviewed Goodall at Cambridge and found him to be a stable and mature person.

In early 1971, Fossey wrote Louis Leakey that she felt confined and alienated at Cambridge. Fossey hated all the formalities there. She felt ill at ease with the people. Leakey wrote back that he planned to visit London in February and would meet her at Cambridge. They would have dinner and a quiet talk.

She was eagerly looking forward to his visit. But shortly after his arrival at the London airport, Dr. Leakey suffered a heart attack and was rushed to a nearby hospital. Fossey took the ninety-minute train ride from Cambridge to visit him during his convalescence. Leakey made a quick recovery and, against the advice of his doctors, continued to work, travel, and lecture nonstop.

The last letter that Fossey received from him arrived a year later while she was at Cambridge. His fund-raising efforts for his varied projects had been unsuccessful; he was having trouble raising money even for his own research. In October 1972 Louis Leakey had a second heart attack. This time it was fatal.

Back Home

Back in the Virungas and with her academic credentials on the way to being secure, Fossey was able to devote more time to being with her gorillas. In 1972, there were 96

Fossey poses for a picture with friends, Mr. and Mrs. Nunyeshyaka, before giving a speech to National Geographic Society members in November 1973.

Nyiramachabelli! Nyiramachabelli!

gorillas in eight family groups living on the fringes of the study area. Dian spent most of her time with Group 4.

In October 1973, Fossey again left Karisoke, this time to undertake a lecture tour of the United States. Following that, she spent her final four months at Cambridge.

It was early in 1974 when Fossey flew back to Africa and returned to Karisoke and her staff. Students and researchers continued to come and go. Fossey trained the new students to keep poachers under control and continued to supervise long-range studies of gorilla groups.

In the early part of 1976, Dian completed her doctoral work and returned to Cambridge.

DR. FOSSEY

In the spring of 1976, Dian Fossey was told that her thesis (the project for her doctoral degree) had been accepted. Although she had never earned a master's degree, her gorilla studies contained so much new information that the examiners awarded her doctorate. She could now be called Dr. Fossey.

From Cambridge, she traveled to California to take part in a symposium—a discussion among experts in a particular field, sponsored by the National Geographic Society. It also featured Jane Goodall and Birute Galdikas, who studied orangutans in Borneo. After a short visit with her mother and stepfather, she returned to Karisoke in late June.

Back at her research station, Fossey sometimes had problems with the graduate students working there. They were not willing to interrupt their observation schedules to cut poachers' snares, and she had confrontations with some of

Dian Fossey (left), Jane Goodall (center), and Birute Galdikas (right) were accomplished field researchers who received encouragement and support from Louis Leakey as they studied primates.

them over the issue. Most disapproved of her war against the poachers. A student named Ian Redmond was one of the few researchers who shared Fossey's preoccupation with stopping poachers. He saw gorillas as she did—as living beings to be understood and cherished on an emotional level as well as an intellectual one. Redmond was 20 years younger than Fossey, and she treated him like a son, with a firm but kind hand. He had no difficulty, as other students did, dealing with her frequent temper tantrums. He often compared them to the charge of a silverback protecting his group.

When Fossey gave a scolding (in a mixture of English, French, and Swahili), people knew exactly what she said.

Nyiramachabelli! Nyiramachabelli!

Dreams Can Come True: The Trimates

Birute Galdikas first met Louis Leakey in March 1969, when Dr. Leakey lectured on primate studies at the University of California at Los Angeles, where Galdikas was a graduate student in anthropology. Immediately following the lecture, Galdikas rushed up to Leakey to tell him that she wanted to do a long-term study of orangutans. Leakey's encouragement and help in raising funds made her dream a reality: In 1971, Galdikas went to Borneo.

In the summer of 1960, Jane Goodall, a 26-year-old English-woman, arrived on the shores of Lake Tanganyika in East Africa. It was unheard of in those days for a young woman to venture into the wilds of Africa. But going to Africa was Goodall's dream, one she had had since childhood. She met Dr. Louis Leakey there. He proposed a field study of chimpanzees in the hopes of gaining insight into our ancient ancestors. Even though Goodall had had no formal scientific training, her strong desire to understand the lives of animals led Leakey to choose her as a pioneer of this pivotal study.

Jane Goodall, Birute Galdikas, and Dian Fossey became the daughters that Dr. Leakey never had. They stood up to him on occasion and sometimes disagreed with him. They became tied to one another like sisters. As Leakey's special "students," they were often called "the trimates"—a play on the word *primates*.

Jane Goodall earned her Ph.D. at Cambridge University in 1965 and has written six major books and numerous articles. Dr. Goodall continues her field studies today, marking more than 35 years of research.

Born in Germany and raised in Canada, Birute Galdikas holds a Ph.D. in anthropology from the University of California at Los Angeles. In addition to chronicling the life cycle of the orangutans in their native habitat in Borneo, she, like Fossey, has battled with poachers. She has also fought illegal trade in infant orangutans. Today, Galdikas divides her time between Borneo, Los Angeles, and Vancouver, Canada, where she teaches at Simon Fraser University.

Dian Fossey's hatred of poachers fired her determination
to keep the gorillas as safe as possible. Here, she leads a
group of trackers into the mountains to search for traps.

At six feet one inch, with piercing dark eyes, she could be
an intimidating presence.

She hated the idea of 20 to 30 tourists being marched up to
see the gorillas by a dozen Batwa tribe members, who would
taunt the animals into beating their chests and screaming.
On one occasion, Fossey even fired shots over the heads of
some uninvited Dutch tourists who had hiked up to
Karisoke.

Her pursuit of poachers continued. Fossey dispatched
teams to trail poachers and reported poaching incidents to
the local police, which would result in a general roundup

Nyiramachabelli! Nyiramachabelli!

of all suspected poachers. In the first 18 months of the campaign, her teams collected about 4,000 snares.

Fossey was becoming dangerous even to herself. She would follow poachers until they made camp and try to scare them off, screaming and firing a pistol in the air.

RETURN TO THE OUTSIDE WORLD

Dian Fossey had other concerns, however. Now that she had her Ph.D., there was increasing pressure to publish her scientific findings. She began to write a book about her life with the gorillas. She also spent two or three days a week in her cabin writing reports, and she kept writing in her journal. Fossey spent as much time as she could spare with her special gorilla friends in Group 4 and took great pleasure in listening to the many creatures in the woods surrounding the Karisoke station.

The Leakey Foundation was also putting pressure on Fossey, threatening to cut off funding if she did not return to the United States to write up her research. She did not want to leave Karisoke; she did not think that anyone else could do the job there as well as she could.

But she seemed to have little choice. In August 1979, Cornell University professor Glenn Hausfater visited Karisoke as part of an African tour he was making to further his studies in primatology. Fossey told him of the Rwandan government's repeated attempts to get her out of Rwanda but said that she had no place to go. Hausfater said that he might have the perfect solution—Fossey might be able to go to Cornell as a visiting professor. Cornell was looking for women scientists to join the faculty, and she seemed a

Fossey and a young gorilla share a quiet moment.
She felt happy spending time with the animals.

perfect candidate. Hausfater promised to do what he could
to get her a teaching position. He was true to his word.

Dr. Fossey accepted a Cornell appointment at a salary of
$13,500 in return for lecturing and teaching a seminar on the

Dian Fossey's Basic Rules for Dealing with Gorillas

- **Never run from a gorilla**
  Gorilla threats are usually bluffs. If you crouch down and focus your eyes on the ground, the gorilla will leave you alone.
- **Never touch a gorilla**
  You can let gorillas touch you, but if you make a move toward them, they may interpret it as an aggressive act.
- **Never surprise a gorilla**
  Let them know you're approaching by humming—"Um-Um-Aah-Um-Um-Aah."
- **Never move suddenly in their presence**
- **Never breathe on a gorilla or visit a group when you're sick**
  A new bacterium or virus could cause an epidemic that would be fatal to this endangered species.
- **Always give a gorilla the right of way**

Warning: According to Rwandan tourist officials, gorilla watchers must be at least 15 years old!

great apes. This schedule would give her the time she needed to finish her book, entitled *Gorillas in the Mist*.

She remained in the United States for three years, but her heart was still in Africa. Indeed, gorillas were her whole life. She often wrote friends that it was only among the gorillas that she could forget her troubles. When she was at Karisoke, she would sit with the gorillas for hours, cuddling and tickling the infants as if they were human children.

In 1983, Fossey returned to Karisoke for good. The years in the United States had been pleasant ones, but there was no permanent place for her there. She had not been successful as a teacher. Fossey's students found her to be aloof and intimidating. Once she was back at Karisoke, Fossey became more of a hermit. The more she worked with the gorillas, the more she preferred being with them to being with people. Her feelings toward gorillas had gone far beyond concern about their survival. Their preservation had become her obsession.

By this time, Fossey was in very poor health. To make the steep and slippery climb to Karisoke, she now had to breathe from an oxygen tank. She was suffering from emphysema, a debilitating illness of the lungs. But she continued to smoke two packs of cigarettes a day. Though she was barely past 50, she talked a lot about retiring, perhaps to a cottage on Lake Kivu, lower down the mountain, with a view of the Virungas.

Karisoke is a beautiful place, with tall hagenia trees scattered throughout the clearing. Fossey did not want visitors walking on the lush green grass, so she marked off a main trail and a few side ones with poles. Her cabin was the largest at the far end of the camp. Researchers lived in corrugated metal huts at the far end of the camp, within earshot of the men's hut, where Karisoke's trackers and anti-poaching patrols lived. There was an open-sided hut where park guards slept.

Fossey called her cabin the "Mausoleum." It had two bedrooms, a living room with an internal brick chimney, a dining room, and a kitchen. Adjoining the kitchen was a locked storeroom filled with old suitcases, boxes, and broken lamps. The cabin also had a front and back porch. Her bedroom was at the rear of the cabin, overlooking two large hagenia trees.

Nyiramachabelli! Nyiramachabelli!

Fossey sits with a group of young gorillas. Gorillas only interact with the people they trust.

The End of the Dream

Wayne McGuire, a 34-year-old American graduate student, arrived to study at Karisoke on the afternoon of August 1, 1985. He immediately went to his cabin, about 50 yards in the other direction, from Dian Fossey's and, exhausted from his long trip, fell fast asleep. The following morning at around 8:30, he was awakened by Fossey shouting, "Hey, McGuire, are you going to spend your next two years inside that cabin?" He opened the door and came face to face with the statuesque Fossey.

"You've heard a lot of bad stories about me," Dian said, "but the best thing to do is ignore them and concentrate on the gorillas."

McGuire had come to Karisoke to do fieldwork required for his Ph.D. from the University of Oklahoma. His objective was to discover whether mature male gorillas, the silverbacks, contributed to the care of infants, and, if they did, whether their attentions had a beneficial effect on the infants' survival. Most of the time, McGuire and Fossey got along fine. They would have dinner together once or twice a month in her cabin.

Fossey's lungs were in bad shape, she limped from a broken leg that had not healed properly, and she appeared thin and frail. She had become, in a way, a prisoner in her own camp. But in spite of her poor health, Fossey had never lost the drive and determination needed to survive on the mountain and protect the mountain gorillas. After Digit had been killed, eight years before, getting rid of poachers had become more important to Fossey than her scientific research on the gorillas. She considered herself the mother of Karisoke gorillas—they were her family, more beloved to her than most people. Protecting them was what she lived for—and what she would die for.

The highlight of Dian Fossey's day came when the tracking and anti-poaching teams reported what had happened in the park, whether or not they had spotted any poachers or their tracks, and which animals they had seen. She was no longer physically able to hike through the forest. In some places here, it was necessary to crawl on one's stomach, and the heavy vegetation would get in the way when walking. One would also have to deal with stinging plants called nettles, which cause burning and itching.

A week after McGuire's arrival at Karisoke, Fossey left for Kigali to renew her visa, as was usual. When she returned a week later, she seemed very upset. She told McGuire that the Rwandan government was trying to take Karisoke away from her. The research center meant a lot to her; she had helped to build every cabin. She was not about to let it be used for tourism or any other commercial purpose. She actually threatened to burn it to the ground before she would let the government have it. She even began to stock up on containers of kerosene.

Two months later, the day was again approaching when Fossey would have to renew her visa. On December 3, she hid her pistols, money, and a few pieces of jewelry behind her lower dresser drawer and left for Kigali. There, to her surprise, the official in charge of immigration told Fossey that she was a cherished guest, that she could remain in Rwanda as long as she wished. He then stamped her passport with a special visa authorizing her to stay in Rwanda for two years. She was ecstatic; she would be able to live at Karisoke and defend the gorillas from any human who might mistreat them. It took her three and a half hours to climb back to camp, stopping often to catch her breath.

As December slipped by, Fossey began to think about Christmas presents. A friend sent her a bamboo picture frame for her color photo of Digit, which she treasured. She began to arrange a small dinner for a Rwandan student, Joseph Munyaneza, who was leaving camp the day after Christmas. She also invited Wayne McGuire. The three exchanged Christmas gifts around the tree. Fossey looked tired and seemed distant. After dinner, McGuire returned to his cabin to type up his notes. Munyaneza left to pack.

Two days later, around 6:30 in the morning, some of the African staff burst into McGuire's cabin, shouting in Swahili, *Dian kufa kufa*—"Dian is dead." Pulling on his longjohns, McGuire followed them to Fossey's cabin, a five-minute walk away. He noticed that a tin sheet on the outer wall of her bedroom had been cut out. Upon entering the house, he saw that it had been ransacked.

The small group stood there in complete shock. Fossey's possessions had been smashed, torn up, and knocked over. Glass from broken kerosene lamps was scattered across the living room floor. Only a Christmas tree remained in place.

McGuire and the others went to Fossey's bedroom. Clothes were hanging out of drawers. The table in the center of the room was overturned. The mattress was pulled halfway off the bed. Fossey's body was lying on the floor, a pistol and a cartridge clip beside her. A brutal gash ran diagonally across her forehead, over the top of her nose, and down her cheek. She had been struck several blows to the top and back of her head with her own panga—a large, broad-bladed knife used for cutting heavy brush or bananas. She had a look of horror on her face.

Whoever killed Dian Fossey must have come in through the wall by tearing a section of the metal sheathing from the southeast corner of her bedroom. Her cabin was always securely locked at night; thus, it must have been cut by someone who knew the cabin layout. Nothing seemed to be missing. Fossey's money and traveler's checks, amounting to about $3,000, plus jewelry, expensive cameras, and other valuable equipment, were untouched.

Karisoke staff members and friends of Dian Fossey lower
her coffin into the ground on December 31, 1985.

Dian Fossey

The Rwandan authorities said that the violent murder of a white person by a Rwandan was unlikely; there had been only one such incident in the past 30 years. The investigators concluded that the murder had been committed by someone who was completely aware of how Karisoke operated. Several people were arrested, but one by one, they were released as they managed to establish their innocence.

The following summer, nine months after Fossey's death, Wayne McGuire was charged with the crime. Told by the American consul, a diplomatic official, that he would soon be arrested, McGuire was warned to leave Rwanda. He was reluctant to go until he had completed his fieldwork for his doctorate, but the consul finally convinced him that it would be in his best interest to leave as soon as possible. On June 27, 1986, McGuire flew to the United States.

As soon as he left Rwanda, an international arrest warrant was issued, charging him and five Rwandans with Fossey's murder. Four of the Rwandans were cleared; the fifth, one of Fossey's trackers, supposedly hanged himself in prison. On December 11, 1986, McGuire was tried *in absentia* (in his absence) by a Rwandan tribunal. They claimed that his motive was the theft of scientific research that Fossey had accumulated over many years. Ten days before the first anniversary of Fossey's death, on December 17, McGuire was convicted of the murder and sentenced to die by a firing squad—that is, if he dared, or was stupid enough, to return to Rwanda.

McGuire has steadfastly maintained his innocence to this day. He claims that he was just a sacrificial lamb—that there was no believable motive and the evidence against him was made up. He argues that it was obvious that someone who was not Rwandan had to take the blame.

Researcher Wayne McGuire was accused by Rwandan officials of killing Dian Fossey. Her killer is still unknown.

Who did kill Dian Fossey? Some suspect that she was murdered by an African she knew, someone who was familiar with Karisoke and the daily routine. Because she was killed with a panga, some believe that she was killed by a poacher seeking vengeance. That person may have been hired by influential people who viewed Fossey as a dangerous obstacle to their using the gorillas for money-making purposes.

Dian Fossey is buried in the gorilla graveyard near her cabin at Karisoke, close to her beloved Digit and the bodies of other gorillas killed by poachers. The tombstone is engraved with her African nickname, *Nyiramachabelli*, "The Woman Who Lives Alone on the Mountain." It reads:

Dian Fossey
1932–1985
No one loved gorillas more.
Rest in peace, dear friend
Eternally protected
In this sacred ground
For you are home
Where you belong.

GORILLAS
IN THE
CROSSFIRE

Some of Dian Fossey's colleagues said that her death was a shock but that they weren't surprised by it, because of the way she treated poachers. Others said that she got what she deserved.

After 1979, gorilla tourism increased in Volcano National Park. The number of guides, guards, and administrators doubled to handle the number of visitors. Local appreciation for the animals also increased, which put significant pressure on poachers to stop harming the gorillas. Many people feel that the credit for this change belongs to Fossey.

As a staff member looks on, Dian Fossey burns poachers' snares. Though her murder remains unsolved, many believe she was killed by poachers.

HER WORK GOES ON

A group of conservationists helped form the Mountain Gorilla Project (MGP) to train guards to protect the wildlife in Rwanda's national parks. The Karisoke Research Center has been in existence for nearly three decades; today, it is administered by the Dian Fossey Gorilla Fund. The fund, established by Dr. Fossey in 1978, was originally called the Digit Fund, in honor of her favorite gorilla. It was renamed in 1992 to strengthen its commitment to carry on gorilla protection and research. Thanks to the MGP and the Fossey Fund, conservation awareness was expanded in Rwandan schools. Educational programs sought to teach school-children and farmers to value the rain forest and its gorillas. Field observations inspired new methods for saving the gorillas from extinction.

Dian Fossey refused to allow the practice of getting some gorillas at Karisoke used to people (habituated) for the sake of tourism. Other researchers, however, felt that making the gorillas "pay for their keep" was the only way to save them for future generations.

Bill Weber, a tropical resource specialist and member of the MGP, began to use Fossey's methods of communication with other gorilla groups. He helped set the stage for "gorilla tourism" by gradually getting two mountain gorilla groups used to the presence of humans. The first encounters were noisy—a silverback would scream, and the whole group would take off running through the forest. But after several more visits, the gorillas began to hold their ground, shrieking at the human intruders, but now mostly for show. Finally, the gorillas came to accept humans. Four gorilla

The Dian Fossey Gorilla Fund works internationally
to protect the endangered mountain gorilla.

groups were habituated in this way. Weber was so success-ful that, in 1987, a Hollywood film crew was able to work with the animals while making the movie *Gorillas in the Mist,* based on Fossey's book.

Shortly afterward, backed by international conservation groups, the MGP launched its tourism program, which it operated in association with the Rwandan government. To prevent overexposure, each gorilla group would be visited by only one tour party a day. Up to 18 tourists in parties of six or less were permitted to hike in the forest, where they spent about one hour among the gorillas, watching and photographing them.

The tourist program, first looked upon with great skepti-cism by Rwandan officials, was very successful. Foreign tourists paid an entrance fee to go into the Volcano National Park to watch the gorillas. Some of the money was used to pay for park protection, and the rest went to the Rwandan government.

Fossey's fear that tourism would disrupt gorillas and side-track efforts to control poaching has so far been unfounded. What about her concern that habituated gorillas, having overcome their natural aversion to humans, would be less likely to shy away from poachers? Researchers say that there is some danger of this but that tourism is still the gorillas' only hope for survival. If people are willing to spend money to watch and photograph gorillas, they reason, the gorillas' habitat—the area where the animals normally live—will be protected. A director of the World Wildlife Fund agrees that there are some risks but thinks that without tourism, there would be increased loss of habitat. Poaching would also continue, resulting in the further reduction of the gorilla population.

CIVIL UNREST

The Rwandan Patriotic Front (RPF) first took up fighting Rwandan government forces in October 1990, and there have been many serious conflicts in the country ever since. Most of the RPF were from the minority Tutsi tribe, who seized control of a small part of northern Rwanda.

Members of the RPF, which had been outlawed since Rwanda won independence from Belgium on July 1, 1962, fled to nearby Uganda and Burundi. They wanted to return to their homeland and participate in the government, which

Diane Doran, director of the Karisoke Research Center in 1990, observes a male mountain gorilla. When RPF fighting reached Karisoke in 1993, the center had to close.

was controlled by the majority Hutu tribe. In February 1993, the RPF gained territory, including control of Volcano National Park.

Once the war between government forces and the RPF reached the northwestern corner of Rwanda, Karisoke's staff had to be evacuated for their own safety. The center was closed down. As a consequence, all of the programs relating to preservation and conservation of the mountain gorilla came to a halt. That was the first time since Dian Fossey had founded Karisoke that all contact with Virunga mountain gorillas was lost.

When members of the RPF arrived at Karisoke, they looted supplies and broke down doors and windows. H. Dieter Steklis, the center's director from 1991 to 1993 and now the chief executive officer of the Dian Fossey Gorilla Fund, which operates Karisoke, said that as far as he knew, the gorillas were left alone. He had been afraid that the gorillas would be shot accidentally during the fighting (one silverback had been shot in the spring of 1992).

The strife brought tourism focusing on gorillas to a halt. This was a huge blow to the country's economy. Gorilla watchers had become Rwanda's third-largest source of foreign income, after coffee and tea. (There are some tours, however, still operating in Zaire and Uganda.)

A cease-fire (a halt to the fighting) was declared in late March 1993. Steklis visited two months later, only to discover that Karisoke had become a camp for poachers. He found evidence that antelope had been shot and the forest cut down. With the help of U.S. Embassy officials, he promptly set about negotiating the return of 13 Karisoke staff members, who resumed anti-poaching patrols and daily contact with the gorillas. The staff lived under the protection of

H. Dieter Steklis led the Karisoke Center
during a turbulent time in Rwanda's history.

armed guards from the Government Parks Office, who
accompanied them on patrols and on gorilla visits.

Negotiations between the Tutsi and Hutu broke down in
June 1993 amid fears of renewed fighting. Both sides assured
the Karisoke staff that they had nothing to fear. The RPF
told Steklis that it was as concerned as anyone else about
the conservation of mountain gorillas, and that it would
like to play a role in protecting the center.

In the spring of 1994, a savage civil war devastated
Rwanda. The fighting claimed more than half a million lives.
The fate of the rare mountain gorillas was also in jeopardy.
By July, the RPF had established a new government and the
violence began to lessen.

Steklis was determined to be the first scientist to return to
the Virunga region to see for himself how the mountain

gorillas had fared during the war. In March 1995, he climbed up the slopes in ankle-deep mud, fighting his way through stinging nettles and deep vegetation. As he edged into a clearing, he signaled his approach with gorillalike grunts. A 400-pound silverback, the patriarch of a clan of 22 gorillas, looked up at him. "I always get emotional when I see them," Steklis said, "but this year it seems like a miracle."

Today the mountain gorillas survive in just two isolated habitats—in Uganda's impenetrable forest and in the Virunga region, which spans the Rwanda, Zaire, and Uganda borders. Happily, it appears that gorillas escaped the immediate effects of the war exploding around them. But threats to this endangered species may still be greater than ever. The biggest threat to the gorillas' habitat has been posed by Rwandans who fled into the forest on their way to refugee camps in Zaire.

Rwandan refugees wait for food in a camp in Zaire. The ongoing civil war has caused many Rwandans to leave their native land.

Land mines and grenades were planted in Volcano National Park by Hutu soldiers as they were ousted from Rwanda by Tutsi rebels in the summer of 1994. It was rumored that a gorilla had been killed by a mine. Hutu soldiers, now in Zaire, make nightly raids across the border into Rwanda and spray automatic rifle fire as they poach animals like buffalo and antelope.

Just two miles away from the Volcano National Park, more than 800,000 Rwandan refugees live in scattered camps in Zaire. As they come back into Rwanda little by little, they travel through the park with long-horned cattle. Not only does this disturb the gorillas' habitat, but it also exposes them to upper respiratory diseases that they have no way of fighting.

The Dian Fossey Gorilla Fund has been in Rwanda for a long time. Since Fossey's murder in 1985, the fund, with its annual budget of $1 million raised from donations of charities and private contributors worldwide, continues to document everything about gorillas—their eating habits, their habitat, their almost human social behavior.

The Survivors

"No mountain gorillas will survive if Rwandans and non-Rwandans don't work together," said Karisoke interim director Peter Clay. But the gorillas are not waiting for humans. They are busy getting on with their own lives. The Karisoke gorillas have produced seven babies since the violent Rwandan summer of 1994. And, despite warnings from Hutu military against returning to work, a group of 25 Hutu and Tutsi rangers and trackers returned to Karisoke to

"Land of a Thousand Hills"

By the 1990s, Rwanda had become the most densely populated country in Africa as well as one of the most impoverished and underprivileged nations in the world. Sandwiched between Tanzania and Zaire in eastern Central Africa, it spans a little over 10,000 square miles in size, roughly comparable to Maryland. The population grew from 3.2 million in the 1960s to more than 8 million by the 1990s. The capital city is Kigali.

Rwanda's first settlers were the Hutu, who make up 90 percent of the population, and the very tall Tutsi (or Watutsi), who make up 9 percent. The Twa, often stereotyped as pygmies, make up the remaining 1 percent. In 1963, one year after Rwanda achieved its independence from Belgium, the Hutu majority cut down the aristocratic Tutsi in a genocidal war.

Rivalries continued between the Hutu and the Tutsi, leading to a bloodless coup in July 1973, when Juvénal Habyarimana came to power as the president of Rwanda. After an invasion and another coup attempt by exiled Tutsi in 1990, a multiparty democracy was established. In August 1993, after continued fighting, there was a peace accord between the government and the rebels of the Tutsi–led Rwandan Patriotic Front (RPF). Sadly, it was not long-lived.

Massive violence broke out after President Habyarimana was killed in a suspicious plane crash on April 6, 1994. More than 200,000 died in massacres as the RPF tried to gain power. The RPF claimed victory and installed a government in July led by a moderate Hutu, President Pasteur Bizimungu. That same year, huge numbers of families fled the terrible violence in Rwanda to the neighboring country of Zaire. They found little food or shelter in the hastily built refugee camps. Many died of cholera and other cruel diseases. Zaire, anxious to see the refugees return to Rwanda, has been negotiating for more than a year with the United Nations High Commissioner for Refugees (UNHCR) to have them readmitted. Those who have returned to Rwanda were pleased to be going home. Most of the repatriated are old, very young, or women, and unlikely to have taken part in the 1994 massacres of Tutsis. For the Rwandan government in Kigali, the repatriation is welcome. "We are delighted to see the refugees coming home," said a grinning Tutsi customs official, "they are our brothers and sisters and we need them to rebuild our country."

A Rwandan soldier surveys the capital city of Kigali on April 13, 1994. With the death of the president, the country erupted in civil war.

Dian Fossey's preservation and conservation
work of the mountain gorilla continues today.

resume their poaching patrols. Poaching has decreased since the war because the RPF makes it difficult to sneak into the park.

Jillian Miller of the London-based Dian Fossey Gorilla Fund noted that the gorilla population survived "seemingly untouched and unaffected" by the war. When one group was disturbed by gunfire, it simply moved about four hours' walking distance away from Karisoke.

Until the brutal civil war in 1994, the gorillas were Rwanda's only claim to international fame. They had attracted thousands of tourists in the two decades since Dian Fossey began publicizing her struggle to stop their extinction by poachers' traps and guns.

Today, the only travelers who visit Rwanda are United Nations peacekeepers, and journalists—hardly more than 15 in one week. The Virungas may still be the most peaceful place in Rwanda. Dian Fossey would be happy to know that Digit's desendants still live where she found her home.

The final entry in Dian Fossey's diary reads: "When you realize the value of all life, you dwell less on what is past and concentrate on the preservation of the future." The mountain gorilla continues to make steady gains—a fitting tribute to the Gorilla Fund and to Dian Fossey's life and work.

Glossary

anthropology The study of human beings and their cultures.

conservation Careful preservation of natural resources.

endangered species A group of animals, plants, or people whose continued existence is threatened.

fossil Remains of a past geological age preserved in the earth.

habitat The place where an animal naturally lives and grows.

habituate To become used to something.

hominid Any of the *Hominidae* family; recent humans, their ancestors, and related forms.

national park A land area that is left wild and is protected by the government. Animals live more safely in a national park.

occupational therapy Therapy using creative activity to promote recovery or rehabilitation from a disease or an accident.

paleoanthropology The study of early hominid fossils.

paleontology The study of extinct animals and plants.

panga A large knife with a broad blade used in Africa to cut objects like thick brush.

poacher Someone who kills or traps wild animals illegally.

primate One of a group of animals that includes monkeys, apes, and humans.

primatology The study of primates.

reserve A tract of public land; an area where hunting is not permitted. Volcano National Park is a reserve.

safari Caravan and equipment of an expedition, especially in East Africa.

species A group of animals or plants whose members can interbreed and produce fertile offspring.

tracker A worker employed to walk over and inspect mountain trails.

tropical rain forest Thick forest in a region where there is heavy rainfall.

zoology A branch of biology concerned with classification, origin, development, and functioning of animals.

Further Reading

Bürgel, Paul Hermann, and Hartwig, Manfred. *Gorillas*. Minneapolis, MN: Carolrhoda Books, 1992.

Fossey, Dian. "Death of Marchessa." *National Geographic*. April 1981.

———. "The Imperiled Mountain Gorilla." *National Geographic*. April 1981.

———. "Making Friends with Mountain Gorillas." *National Geographic*. January 1970.

———. "More Years with Mountain Gorillas." *National Geographic*. October 1971.

Jerome, Leah. *Dian Fossey*. New York: Bantam Skylark, 1991.

Redmond, Ian. *Gorillas*. (Wildlife at Risk Series) New York: Franklin Watts, 1991.

Schlein, Miriam. *Jane Goodall's Animal World: Gorillas*. New York: Macmillan Child Corporation, 1990.

Sources

Fossey, Dian. *Gorillas in the Mist.* Boston: Houghton Mifflin, 1983.

"Gorillas Versus Guerrillas." *Audubon.* September/October 1993.

Hayes, Harold T. P. *The Dark Romance of Dian Fossey.* New York: Simon and Schuster, 1990.

"High Above It All." *Macleans.* February 6, 1995.

McGuire, Wayne. "I Didn't Kill Dian, She Was My Friend." *Discover.* February 1987.

Mowat, Farley. *Woman in the Mists.* New York: Warner Books, 1987.

National Geographic Society. *The Great Apes Between Two Worlds.* Washington, D.C.: National Geographic Society, 1993.

"The Poachers' Revenge." *Outside.* May 1986.

Schaller, George. *The Year of the Gorilla.* Chicago: University of Chicago Press, 1964.

"Survivors in the Mist." *People Weekly.* March 6, 1995.

"Up Close with Gorillas." *International Wildlife.* November/December 1988.

Where to Write for More Information

The Mountain Gorilla Project
c/o African Wildlife Foundation
1717 Massachusetts Avenue, NW
Washington, D.C. 20036

Dian Fossey Gorilla Fund
800 Cherokee Avenue, SE
Atlanta, GA 30315-5925

Wildlife Conservation Society
The Wildlife Conservation Park
Bronx, NY 10460

World Wildlife Fund
1255 23rd Street, NW
Washington, D.C. 20037

INDEX

Boldfaced, italicized page numbers include picture references.